Coffee its History, Cultivation, and Uses

COFFEE:

TS HISTORY, CULTIVATION,

AND USES.

By ROBERT HEWITT, Jr.

ILLUSTRATED WITH ORIGINAL DESIGNS BY EMINENT AMERICAN ARTISTS,
AND A MAP OF THE WORLD SHOWING THE SEVERAL PLACES WHERE
COFFEE IS, OR MAY BE PRODUCED, AND WHERE IT IS ALSO
USED

NEW YORK:
D. APPLETON AND COMPANY,
549 & 551 BROADWAY.
1872.

4

TO

Benjamin G. Arnold, Esquire,

WHOSE

MERCANTILE ABILITY AND HONORABLE DEALING

ENTITLE HIM TO

THE FIRST RANK AND POSITION

IN THE

COFFEE TRADE,

This Work is Respectfully Inscribed

BY THE AUTHOR.

CONTENTS.

PREFACE.

THE reader may possibly remember among the charming "*Essays of Elia*" one entitled "A Dissertation on roast Pig," in which the writer, with true epicurean zest, insists upon its preferred claims. Whether the reader's taste be in exact accord with that of the essayist, it may not be easy to determine; but who can fail of being delighted with his treatment of the subject? It is with some such feeling of enthusiastic interest that the present volume has been prepared, and in a similar spirit it is now submitted to the candor of the reader. If occasion for enthusiasm is found in discussing the merits of roasted pig, surely very much stronger is the argument in behalf of roasted Coffee.

Having from his earliest business associations been personally connected with the Coffee-trade, the writer has always been greatly interested in collecting anything relating to the history, cultivation, or uses of this great staple. Long impressed with the idea that the mass of statistical figures that accumulate from day to day, in the many circulars and market reports received by those engaged in the importation and sale of coffee, tend rather to confuse and detract from the importance of this constantly increasing branch of commerce, the following pages are intended to give such general information as may perhaps interest not only those who are familiar with the business, but also that multitudinous class to whom coffee now has become an indispensable beverage;

but who for the most part may not be familiar with its history and production. In a word, the work seeks to present, in a concise yet comprehensive form, all that relates to the history and cultivation of coffee in various countries, and the pernicious effects of its adulteration. The best authorities have been consulted in its preparation; and it is to be hoped—since it has been compiled in response to repeated inquiries for some such a manual, by persons engaged in the coffee-trade—that it may be found acceptable.

As it would be great temerity on his part, after what has been already stated, to bespeak for the volume any special literary merit, its claims upon the favor of the reader must depend mainly upon the intrinsic value of its statements and facts; its typographic and pictorial character will bear its own comment. "After many erasures, interlinings, enlargings, and diminishings," it is at last completed, and, as it is the first attempt of a novice, it is deemed right and proper to say (in strictest confidence) that his vocation is simply that of a coffee-broker, one of that numerous fraternity whose business it is to please both buyer and seller, and who should be informed not only as to the present crop, but, to satisfy *some*, should have an opinion, when it is called for, as to all coming crops, etc., when chatting in the odd moments pending so momentous a transaction as a purchase or a sale (quantity not defined) of coffee. In fine, worthy reader, having thus far detained thee with a relation of the intent and purpose of the following pages, it only remains, by thy courtesy, to venture the hope that what is now presented concerning the little aromatic berry may linger as pleasantly on thy mind and memory as a fragrant draught of its infusion does upon thy palate.

ROBERT HEWITT, JR.

"Coffee! oh, Coffee! Faith, it is surprising,
   'Mid all the poets, good and bad and worse,
Who've scribbled (Hock or Chian eulogizing)
   Post and papyrus with 'immortal verse,'—
Melodiously similitudinizing
   In Sapphics languid, or Alcaics terse,—
No one, my little brown Arabian berry,
   Hath sung *thy* praises,—'tis surprising, very!"

Is not the very name, COFFEE, suggestive of aromatic odors? Is it not, indeed, the fragrant incense we proffer at the shrine of the social hearth,—the delicious libation which we pour on the altar of friendship? Talk of the famed Falernian wine of the ancients, or the nectar and ambrosia of the gods; what were they to a delectable

1*

draught of this world-renowned decoction? Is it not the luxurious accompaniment of the chibouk and the cigar, and one of
the indispensable symbols of the hospitalities and amenities of
life? Yes, better far than the Bacchanalian cup of old is
this non-inebriating draught, since it may be indulged with
impunity;—for while it refreshes and stimulates, it does not
stultify the mind. Wine, doubtless, inspired the ancient muse,
and not, indeed, the ancient poets only; and poetry, which
has been styled "the wine of the mind," was put into competition, in olden time, for the prize of a cask of wine; while
the Bacchic hymn was styled the "hymn of the cask." The
poets-laureate have also, from the minstrel-monk, Chaucer,
down to their living representative in England, continued to
receive their "pipe of wine;" from all which it seems that the
bards do not *solely* seek inspiration from the Heliconian fount!
As a salutary beverage coffee has never, perhaps, been duly
estimated, since it is not only a digestive drink, but it has
suppressed to a great extent that excessive indulgence in
inebriating draughts, that so frequently dishonored the ban-
quets and prodigal hospitalities of former times.

> " Yes, the wine's a wayward child,—
> *This* the cup that 'draws it mild!'
> Deeply drink its stream divine,
> Fill the cup—but not with wine,—
> Potent port, or fiery sherry;—
> For this milder cup of mine,
> Crush me Yemen's fragrant berry!"

Not alone in the East is the amber beverage indispensable;
it has also become a positive necessity in all the great capitals
of Europe, as well as with all classes throughout the length and
breadth of our own land. It has been well said by a recent
writer, in one of our leading periodicals,—"that the proud son
of the highest civilization can no longer live happily without
the coffee of African robbers, the tobacco of the red barbarians,

the tea of the despised Chinese, and the sugar of the wretched
Hindoo or enslaved negro. He cannot break his fast without
coffee, nor finish his dinner; and the whole social life of many
nations is based upon the insignificant bean." The magic
drink, which has held such unlimited sway over the social
hospitalities of mankind for centuries, has also ministered to
the relief of innumerable despairing dyspeptics, and achieved
an incalculable amount of good, in rendering people more
happy, and on better terms with themselves and everybody
else, as well as more thoroughly equipped for encountering
the battle of life. It is also suggestive of pleasant memories
and visions of joyous, smiling groups that have graced the
festive board, and shared with ourselves those genial "moods
and tenses" that constitute much of the poetry of life. If the
dreamy Mohammedan delights to divide his hours between the
rival fascinations of his fragrant cup and the aroma of his
"witching weed" in solemn silence, we of the Western World
find in this favorite beverage a delightful auxiliary to some of
our purest *social* pleasures. Its influence upon the social
habits and intellectual culture of the age is a beneficent one,
for it not only exhilarates the mind, but it also acts as a gentle
stimulant, recuperative and sustaining to the physical frame.
Since cotton has been proclaimed "king" in the realm of commerce, coffee should be styled "queen" among the beverages
of domestic life. True, tea takes prominent rank with many
of the gentler sex, yet its fair fame has been traditionally
suggestive of a love of scandal; while the aromatic berry is
wholly free from such a stigma. Had the learned lexicogra
pher been less prodigal in his use of tea, and indulged himself
with a frequent cup of fragrant coffee, he doubtless would
have exhibited less asperity and angularity of character, and
might have become as genial as he was wise. Like coffee,
tobacco is also a potent plant:—both alike hold absolute sway

over millions of mankind; yet, yielding too freely to the seductive influence of the narcotic weed, we may have to suffer the penalty, while with the aromatic berry nature is rarely in revolt. The one stimulates but to enervate; the other refreshes and sustains. Coffee also is a better disinfectant than tobacco.

In the olden time, when the " occult sciences," so called, were in vogue with the learned as well as the superstitious, women indulged implicit faith in omens, premonitions, and " signs " In Brande's " Antiquities," allusion is made to a curious species of divination by, or tossing of, coffee-grounds. The narrator relates a visit he paid to a lady ;—" whom he surprised with her company in close cabal over their coffee, the rest very intent upon one whom by her address and intelligence he guessed was a tire-woman, to which she added the secret of divining by coffee-grounds. She was then in full inspiration, and with much solemnity observing the atoms around the cup; on the one hand sat a widow, on the other a maiden lady. . . . They assured him that every cast of the cup is a picture of all one's life to come, and every transaction and circumstance is delineated with the exactest certainty," etc. The same practice is also noticed in the *Connoisseur*, where a girl is represented divining to find out of what rank her husband should be :—" I have seen him several times in *coffee-grounds*, with a sword by his side; and he was once at the bottom of a tea-cup, in a coach-and-six, with two footmen behind it! "

Leigh Hunt thus pleasantly discourses upon our subject: " Coffee, like tea, used to form a refreshment by itself, some hours after dinner; it is now taken as a digester, right upon that meal or the wine, and sometimes does not even close it; or the digester itself is digested by a liqueur of some sort called a *chasse-café* (coffee-chaser). We like coffee better than tea for the taste, but tea ' for a constancy.' To be perfect in point of relish (we do not say of wholesomeness), coffee should be strong and hot, with little milk and sugar. It has been drunk after this mode in some parts of Europe, but the public have nowhere, we believe, adopted it.   The favorite way of taking it as a meal, abroad, is with a great superfluity of milk—very properly called, in France, *café-au-lait* (coffee *to the* milk). One of the pleasures we receive in drinking coffee is that, being the universal drink in the East, it reminds of that region of the ' Arabian Nights,' as smoking does for the same reason; though neither of these refreshments, which are identified with Oriental manners, is to be found in that enchanting work. They had not been discovered when it was written; the drink then was sherbet.   One can hardly fancy what a Turk or a Persian could have done without coffee and a pipe, any more than the English ladies and gentlemen, before the civil wars, without tea for breakfast."

Thus much, then, may suffice as our " apology " for proposing to the reader to accompany us in our rapid survey of the career of coffee over the globe, since its first discovery. What we have here gleaned from a great variety of sources concerning the fragrant berry, has been to the compiler by no means a theme devoid of interest; but should the reader not be of the same opinion, it may not be inappropriate to suggest that, before committing to him the results of our researches, he should fortify himself with a cup of the inspiring beverage, and thus be put into true sympathy with the subject.

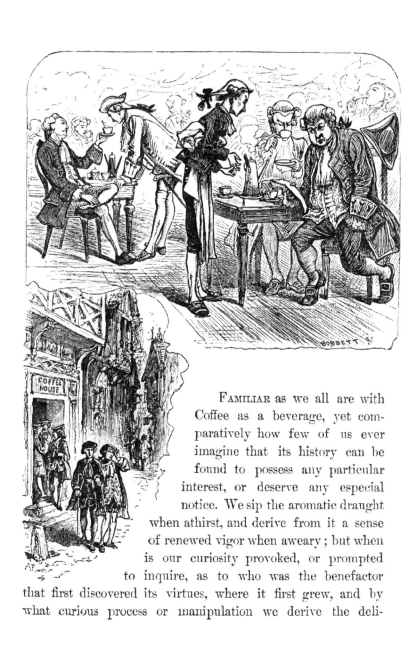

FAMILIAR as we all are with
Coffee as a beverage, yet comparatively how few of us ever
imagine that its history can be
found to possess any particular
interest, or deserve any especial
notice. We sip the aromatic draught
when athirst, and derive from it a sense
of renewed vigor when aweary; but when
is our curiosity provoked, or prompted
to inquire, as to who was the benefactor
that first discovered its virtues, where it first grew, and by
what curious process or manipulation we derive the deli-

cious drink ' Everything has, indeed, its history or tradition, and so has the fragrant little berry, the aromatic incense of which so gratefully greets our olfactory nerve, at the repast which ushers in the dawn and close of day.

Coffee, it appears, became known to civilization at an epoch memorable for many marvellous events. It was about the time of the great awakening of mankind from the long slumbers of the Middle Ages, when those great luminaries, Columbus and Faust, blazed upon the world. One brought to light a new hemisphere, and the other gave to mankind the " art preservative of arts," and the light of intelligence to the whole civilized globe. Coffee was originally known by the name of *Kauhi*, an orthography somewhat suggestive of a certain Town Councillor of Leeds, who, writing out a "bill of fare" for a public breakfast, contrived to spell *coffee* without employing a single letter that occurs in that word, thus—*Kawphy!* Although the plant or tree is indigenous to Southern Abyssinia, where it is even to the present day cultivated, yet it derived its name from *Kaffa*, in Eastern Africa, where the plant also grows wild, and very abundantly. The Malays, who from their intercourse with the Arabs have long known the berry, call it by the Arabian name, *Kawah;* the Javanese, however, in common with ourselves, designate it Coffee. There is an Eastern legend which ascribes the discovery of the berry to a Dervish named Hadji Omer, who, in the year 1285, being driven out of Mocha, was induced, in the extremity of hunger, to roast the berries which grew near his hiding-place. He ate them, as the only means of sustaining life; and steeping the roasted berries in water, to quench his thirst, he thus discovered their agreeable qualities, and also that the infusion was nearly equal to solid food. His persecutors, who had intended that he should die of starvation, regarded his preservation as a miracle. He was accordingly transmuted into a saint forthwith !

According to the manuscript of Schehabeddin Ben, an Arabian Scribe of the ninth century of the Hegira, or the fifteenth of the Christian era, which manuscript is, or was, in the great Library of the city of Paris, we learn that a certain Mufti, or Mohammedan high-priest, named Gemal Eddin, of Aden, a town of Arabia Felix, was the first who introduced to his countrymen the custom of coffee-drinking. Having returned from visiting Persia, where he had observed the beverage used as a medicine, and being at the time himself sick, he tried as an experiment a dose of the "black draught." Finding it both curative and exhilarating, he forthwith turned his discovery to good account, by applying its virtues as an antidote to the torpor and drowsiness of his monks, whom he had often found dormant at their devotions.

The example and authority of the Mufti at once conferred on coffee a reputation, and it speedily came into general use, not only on account of its sleep-dispelling power, but also for its other good qualities. Coffee, which had been in use in Ethiopia, it is believed, from time immemorial, was carried by the Dervishes to Mecca, where the beverage became so popular with the sons of the prophet that its fame soon extended to other towns adjacent. It continued its career through Syria, and was received without opposition at Damascus and Aleppo, and in the year 1554 became the favorite drink at Constantinople, where, soon after, coffee-houses were opened.

In the same proportion that the coffee-houses were thronged, the mosques became deserted; and the priests represented that no doubt the new drink was forbidden by the Koran, for that the roasted berry was certainly a kind of coal, and that as such it was prohibited by the Prophet's law. The Mufti, on a petition to this effect, without hesitation decided that coffee was coal; nevertheless, in spite of frequent enactments against it, the people continued to drink it. The exertions of the police were

ineffectual, and the government was at length contented to re-
strain its use merely by rigid sumptuary laws. Coffee was
taxed, and the black draught was allowed to be drunk in secret
But ere long another Mufti arose, of a less antiphlogistic turn,
and he pronounced coffee not coal, but a right remunerative
item of government tax. At a later day, when too much free-
dom of political discussion took place in the Oriental coffee-
houses, they were suppressed by the Grand Vizier; yet the
beverage continued to be almost universally used, some persons
taking even twenty dishes of it in a day—the dishes, however,
were small   The lower classes also actually begged money for
coffee; and it is added by the chronicler of the time, that "the
refusing to supply a wife with coffee was admitted in law as a
valid cause of divorce." From the "city of the Sultan" it passed
to Western Europe, but at what precise time, historians have
not positively determined   It is believed to have been introduced into Venice about the year 1615.   In 1644 it was known
at Marseilles, M. de la Haye having taken with him some of the
coffee-beans from Constantinople, with vessels and an apparatus
for making the beverage.

The traveller Thevenot was among the first to introduce into
Paris the custom of taking coffee after dinner , but he had few
imitators until ten years after,—about 1668, when the coffee
parties of the Turkish ambassador at Paris brought the beverage into fashion.   "The brilliant porcelain cups," says Disraeli,
"in which it is poured,—the napkins fringed with gold, and the
Turkish slaves, on their knees, presenting it to the ladies, seated on the ground on cushions,—turned the heads of the Parisian
dames," the exotic soon became a subject of general conversation, and a *café* was opened for the sale of the beverage, in
1671, by an Armenian of the name of Pascal.   The enterprise
did not succeed, however, on account of the heterogeneous company that met there.   A few years later, Procope, a Florentine,

who became noted as an arbiter of taste in such matters, opened a splendid saloon, at which the rank and fashion of the French capital used to assemble.

Soon the *café* became the resort of the most renowned wits, artists, and philosophers of the French metropolis—Rousseau, Voltaire, Piron, with Marmontel and many others. The universal favor in which coffee is still held in Paris, sufficiently disproves the accuracy of the famous prophecy of Madame de Sévigné,—that "coffee and Racine would have their day." Among the most noted of the Parisian *cafés* were those known as the *Café des Mille Colonnes*, and the *Café Turc*, on the Boulevard, which were fitted up with oriental splendor, as glittering with ornament as an opium-eater's dreams, or the glowing tints of a page of *Vathek*.

The high favor with which coffee came at length to be regarded in the houses of the great, may be inferred from the fact that a sum equivalent to $15,000 a year was expended for supplying the daughters of Louis XV. of France with the beverage. In 1714 the magistrates of Amsterdam presented Louis XIV. with a coffee-tree, which was sent to the Royal Gardens. It was Louis XIV. who directed M. Des Clieux to take one of the plants to Martinique, one of the French West India possessions. The voyage proved so tempestuous and prolonged that he was compelled to divide his water-rations with it, in order to keep it alive. From that parent plant an immense progeny has sprung.

The consumption of coffee in the French capital at the breaking out of the Revolution was something enormous. We find it estimated that the French West India Islands furnished no less than eighty millions of pounds of it yearly, and this was, irrespective of a liberal supply from the East. The two sources combined were not even adequate to the supply of the demand. We are not surely to infer from this circumstance that coffee itself possesses any Revolutionary element.

It was to this extraordinary demand for coffee that the adulterations of the berry may be traced;—the adulterers made fortunes by their combination of chiccory with it, but the well-earned reputation of the French suffered by the admixture.

At the " Café Procope," the earliest of these establishments in Paris, a curious incident, worth mentioning, occurred concerning a cup of coffee. As M. Saint Foix was one day seated at his usual table in this café, an officer of the king's body-guard entered, sat down, and ordered a cup of coffee, with milk and a roll, adding, " It will serve me for a dinner ! " At this Saint Foix remarked aloud, " that a cup of coffee, with milk and a roll, was a confoundedly poor dinner." The officer remonstrated. Saint Foix reiterated his remark, adding, that nothing he could say to the contrary would convince him that it was *not* a confoundedly poor dinner. Thereupon a challenge was given and accepted, and the whole company present adjourned as spectators of a fight, which ended by Saint Foix receiving a wound in the arm. " That is all very well," said the wounded combatant, " but I call you to witness, gentlemen, that I am still profoundly convinced that a cup of coffee, with milk and a roll, is a confoundedly poor dinner ! " At this moment the principals were arrested and carried before the Duke de Noailles, in whose presence St. Foix, without waiting to be questioned, said, " Monseigneur, I had not the slightest intention of offending the gallant officer, who, I doubt not, is an honorable man, but your Excellency can never prevent my asserting that a cup of coffee, with milk and a roll, is a confoundedly poor dinner."—" Why, so it is," said the Duke. " Then I am not in the wrong," persisted St Foix, " and a cup of coffee,"—at these words magistrates, delinquents, and auditory burst into a roar of laughter, and the antagonists became forthwith warm friends The oldest café in the Palais Royal is the celebrated " Café de Foy," so called from the name of its founder. Carl Vernet was one of its most constant patrons. He was there on one occasion when some repairs were going on, and in his impatience he flung a wet coloring-brush from him which struck the ceiling and left a spot. He immediately ascended the ladder, and with a touch of his finger converted the stain into a swallow; and his handi-work was to be seen until the recent siege of Paris. It was before this café that Desmoulins harangued the mob, in July, 1789, with such effect that they took up arms, destroyed the Bastille, and inaugurated the fearful scenes of the Revolution. The Germans were initiated into the practice of coffee-drinking by their neighbors the French, and also by the Dutch. The beverage did not, however, become popular with them until the Elector of Brandenburg caused its virtues and praises to be celebrated in a book, which he disseminated among the people. We have already spoken of the devotion of the Turk to this drink, now almost the universal beverage of the East. It is difficult to transfer ourselves in thought and feeling to the glowing scenes of the Orient. Imagine yourself peering into one of the brilliant divans of the " City of the Sultan," with its tessellated court-yard, and its towering pinnacle or minaret, nestled among mulberry trees and pomegranates. In the cen-tre of the richly decorated saloon is the cooling fountain, which scatters its silvery spray and fantastic foam over groups of bril-liant flowers, while on every side the eye is regaled with varie-gated marbles, magnificent arabesques, and gaudy hangings, relieved with gilded devices of matchless beauty. In some such circumstances of luxurious splendor may be seen the indolent Osmanli regaling himself with his favorite weed, and a cup of his unmixed Mocha silently brought to him by his Nubian slave, in brilliant costume   Among the surrounding groups are some Arabs at chess, while others may be listening to one of the famous Oriental story-tellers, or gazing at the tricks of some juggler, or witnessing the exploits of a dancing dervish. But

silence, indolence, and stolidity are the prevailing characteristics of the Turkish divan. In Persia, however, the scene is
changed; there the coffee-houses are full of stir and activity.
Soon after morning prayers are announced from the minaret, the
people flock to their coffee-houses, which are often beautifully
decorated, and there they sip their coffee, smoke, and listen to
the wise sayings of Sadi, or the songs of Hafiz, or talk over the
news of the hour.

Those who have visited the Havana and roamed through
that delightful city will remember with pleasurable sensations
the magnificent cafés, and especially the "Louvre." Sauntering
from the city gates, where the white-clad officials, with Panama
hats, demand from all travellers landing from the steamers a
silver fee for permission to remain a certain number of days
upon the island, the "looker-on at Vienna" strolls through the
lovely "Plaza de Armas" with its fountains and its flowers;
halts for a few moments on the paved walks, and while listening to the music of the military band, admires the beautiful
faces and graceful toilets of the fair promenaders, who pass
and repass under the lamps, enjoying the tropical twilight.
Taking a victoria, which is the popular vehicle always to be
found ready to convey passengers to any part of the city, he is
whirled past the palace of the Governor-General, and through
narrow streets, between the massive walls of houses on either
side, until he alights at the "Louvre." This café is situated
opposite the Tacon theatre, which is known for its elegance
of construction and rich appointments. Facing it is a
splendid park, used as a promenade during the evening,
when it is brilliantly illuminated. It is the fashionable resort
for promenaders The scene is worth witnessing, presenting
a changing panorama of brilliant variety, while richly appointed equipages, volantes and other vehicles, all gayly
equipped, are constantly passing.

Leaving the victoria, which has by this time obtained another fare, the café with its open doors attracts attention. Entering the grand saloon on the first floor, level with the narrow sidewalks, which permit only one pedestrian to pass comfortably at a time, the visitor seats himself at one of the small marble-covered tables that are plentifully distributed over the tiled floor; and whatever the temperature of the streets may be, the cafés are always cool, and at them may be met, at certain hours of the day, many English and American visitors and residents. Immediately when seated, one of the attendants approaches and politely asks, in Spanish, for orders; an attempt to make the waiter comprehend English will generally meet with signal failure. While enjoying the delicious coffee and a choice cigar, the visitor looks about the saloon, which is fitted up in a style of magnificence out-rivalling all other cafés in the city. At each of the small tables are groups of Spaniards, Cubans, Germans, Englishmen, and Americans, with here and there an officer in brilliant uniform, all chatting, drinking coffee, or sipping light wines, and each, with rare exceptions, fondling a cigar. All over this interesting city, more especially in the older portion of it, inside the now nearly obliterated lines of ancient walls, the cafés confront the passer-by at nearly every square. Watching an old coffee-drinker in the "Louvre" one day, he was seen to carefully drop the white lumps of sugar into his cup until the top of the sweet pile rose just above the rich yellow fluid, and then gently rubbing his palms together, he prepared himself to enjoy the nectar. "La Dominica" was formerly the favorite café, but it has of late years been superseded by more modern establishments; it is still however well patronized, but makes more of a specialty in manufacturing "dulces" or sweetmeats, which have a world-wide reputation, especially the guava jelly, most of which comes from this entrepôt. The Havanese understand pretty well how to make and drink coffee, and never hesitate to avail themselves of its invigorating influence. When dwellers in the tropics—not only in this delightful island but wherever coffee is grown—once learn how to make coffee in perfection, which can only be done by steam-heat, a new impetus will be given to the growth of the bean, for, like all discoveries of value, the better an article is produced, the more universally is it used.

Coffee was first regularly introduced into England about the middle of the seventeenth century, as we learn from the following extract from Sir Henry Blount, who visited Turkey in 1634:—"The Turks have a drink," he writes, "called *Cauphè*, made of a berry as big as a small bean, dried in a furnace, and beat to a powder of a sooty color, in taste a little bitterish, that they seethe and drink, hot as may be endured. It is good at all hours of the day, but especially at morning and evening, when to that purpose they entertain themselves two or three hours in cauphè-houses, which, in Turkey, abound more than Inns and ale-houses with us." Notwithstanding the opposition and prejudice which prevailed against the beverage for nearly a score of years after its first introduction, the coffee-houses continued to increase in London and other large cities of England. All classes resorted to them; literary men and artists, mercantile men and the votaries of fashion, all had their respective coffee-houses. Thus—

> "Mocha's berry, from Arabia pure,
> In small, fine, china cups came in at last."

The English and French dispute the honor of being the first introducers of coffee into Western Europe. Coffee was not used at Rome until long after it had been known to, and tasted by, Italian travellers at Constantinople; the Church, however, looked with favor upon a beverage, one effect of which was to keep both priests and people awake. Although the coffee-houses of England take precedence of those of France, yet the latter have more enduringly flourished. On the authority of Oldys, the antiquary, " the first use of coffee in England was known in 1657, when one Edwards, a Turkey merchant, brought from Smyrna to London one Pasqua Rosee, a Ragusan youth, who prepared this drink for him every morning. But the novelty thereof drawing too much company to him, he allowed his said servant, with another of his sons-in-law, to sell it publicly; and they set up the first coffee-house in London, in St. Michael's Alley, Cornhill. But they separating, Pasqua kept in the house; and he who had been his partner obtained leave to pitch a tent, and sell the liquor, in St. Michael's Churchyard." Aubrey, in his " Anecdotes," states that the first vender of coffee in London was one Bowman, coachman to a Turkey merchant named Hodges, who was the father-in-law of Edwards, and the partner of Pasqua, who got into difficulties, partly by his not being a freeman, and who left the country. Bowman was not only patronized, but a magnificent contribution of one thousand sixpences was presented to him, wherewith he made great improvements in his coffee-house. Bowman took an apprentice (Paynter), who learned the mystery of coffee-making, and soon after set up for himself. The coffee-houses, after this, soon became numerous.

The frequenters of coffee-houses, however, were not then regarded as belonging to the most reputable classes of society, and the proposed substitution of a cup of the Arabian infusion for Canary wine, provoked the opposition of the wits and satirists. The ladies, also, declared against its being thus sold at coffee-houses,—from which they were excluded,—as being unsocial and uncivil. On the other hand, apologists and advocates were not wanting in their behalf: one of the most curious of which was that of Aubrey,—the Boswell of his day,—who declared that he should never have acquired so extensive an acquaintance but for the "modern advantages of coffee-houses in this great city; before which men knew not how to be acquainted but with their own relations and societies!"

An animated controversy was kept up about coffee during the sixteenth and seventeenth centuries. Among the squibs and lampoons of the time may be mentioned the following piquant titles:—"*The Coffee-house Granado*," "*The Women's Petition against Coffee*," and "*The Men's Answer to the same*." Another was entitled, "*A cup of Coffee, or Coffee in its true Colour:*" and a grave writer in prose issued a grotesque hand-bill, headed with a rude cut of coffee-bibbers, surrounded with the following eulogistic legend: "A brief description of the excellent vertues of that sober and wholesome drinke, called coffee, and its incomparable effects in preventing or curing most diseases incidental to human bodies!" When first introduced into London, coffee sold at from four to five guineas a pound. In spite of opposition, coffee soon became a favorite drink, and the shops where it was sold, places of general resort! Another of the earliest coffee-houses of London was the well-known "Rainbow," near Temple Bar, which still flourishes, but altogether in a new style. In 1675 a proclamation was issued for closing all coffee-houses. The government soon found, however, that in making such a proclamation they had gone a step too far; for the coffee-houses of even that day had become a "power in the land." They were indeed the chief organs through which the public opinion of the metropolis was expressed That coffee-houses in Charles the Second's time were regarded as headquarters for the news of the day, we gather from a "broadside" song, which commences thus:—

" You that delight in wit and mirth, and long to hear such news
As come from all parts of the earth,—Dutch, Danes, and Turks, and Jews ;—
I'll send you to a rendezvous, where it is smoking new ;
And coming from the coffee-house, it cannot but be true ! "

Doran, in his amusing volume, " Table Traits," has gathered
some curious items and incidents connected with the old London
coffee-houses which are replete with interest, and which we
shall condense for the reader. The " Grecian" was one of the
most noted of the old establishments of this kind in London ;
it appears to have been the oldest of the better-known of the
coffee-houses, and to have lasted the longest. It was opened by
one Constantine, a Greek, living in the latter part of the seventeenth century, and its location was in the vicinity of St Christo-
pher's Church. Its longevity is not a little remarkable, for its
career came to a close only in the year 1843, when the "Grecian
Coffee-house" became transformed into the "Grecian Chambers,"
or lodgings for bachelors. The establishment did not exist in the
same locality, however, all the time ; for at the time of its
transformation the " Grecian " was situated in Devereux Street,
Strand. In its palmy days it was the resort of the learned
and aristocratic, and its classic name seems not to have been
dishonored by its fame. Sparkling humor and genial repartee
would often flash responsive to the inspiring but non-inebriating
cup, and thus qualify the gravity of those learned pundits who
would gather there, not to discuss the trivialities of the day, but
those weightier matters that concern the rise and fall of dy-
nasties,—such as the fate of Rome and the events which issued
from the Trojan war. Yet then, as now, satirists would seize
upon the points of humor ; and as there were pedants as well
as philosophers who convened at the " Grecian," so lampoons
and literary squibs were not wanting to enliven the scene.

It was a time when both sages and sciolists wore swords ;
and it is on record that two friendly scholars, sipping their

coffee at the " Grecian," became enemies in argument, the subject of which was the accent of a Greek word. Whatever the accent ought to have been, the quarrel was *acute*, and its conclusion *grave*. The scholars rushed into Devereux Court, drew their swords, and as one was run through the body and killed on the spot, it is to be supposed that he was necessarily wrong A duel, however, was certainly a strange way of settling a question in grammar. The " coffee-houses " which were resorted to for mere conversation as well as coffee began on a first floor ; they were the seed, as it were, whence has arisen the political and exclusive " club " of the present day. The advantages of association were first experienced in coffee-houses ; but at the same time it must be admitted that there also was felt the annoyance caused by intrusive and unwelcome strangers. " Wills's Coffee-house," also known as the " Wits " from its company, was situated at the west corner of Bow Street, Covent Garden. In the last half of the seventeenth century, its popularity was at its height It was at Wills's that Dryden " pedagogued " without restraint, and accepted without a blush any amount of flattery on his literary productions. He was the great literary luminary around which lesser orbs and satellites revolved. He had the good sense, however, to retire early, when the tables were full, and he knew he had made a favorable impression ; but Addison, more given to jolly fellowship, sat late with those who stayed to indulge " libations deep." Of the disputes that there arose, " Glorious John " was arbiter : for his particular use a chair was especially reserved ; therein enthroned he sat by the hearth or the balcony, according to the season, and delivered his decisions. Another of the renowned London coffee-houses was " Button's," in Great Russell Street ; this was Addison's favorite rendezvous, although the fruit of the vine was, in his case, preferred to the infusion of the berry. There, after writing during the forenoon at his house in

St. James's Place,—where his breakfast table was attended by
such men as Steele, Davenant, Carey, Philips, Pope, and other
bards and writers of note,—he was to be found of an evening until
supper.   Pope was of the company for about a year, but left it
partly because late hours injured his health, and partly also
because his irritable temper had rendered him unpopular.   He
had so provoked Ambrose Philips, indeed, that the latter sus-
pended a birchen-rod over Pope's usual seat, in intimation of
what the ordinary occupant would get if he ventured into it.
The Buttonians were famous for the fierceness of their criti-
cism.   Of coffee-houses that went by the name of " Tom's "
there were three : at that in Birchen-lane Garrick frequently
might have been seen ; and poor Chatterton, before fell despair
slew him.   At the other coffee-house known as " Tom's," in
Devereux Court, Akenside, with many of the scholars, critics,
and scientists of the day used to congregate ; but *the* " Tom's "
was opposite Button's, in Great Russell Street.   It was a place
generally crowded with incident, from the time of Queen Anne
to that of George III.   Seven hundred of the nobility, literary
notabilities, and wits of celebrity were guinea subscribers to
this establishment ; most of the company, however, consoled
themselves with something more potent than coffee.   The politicians as well as the poets had their coffee-houses ; the " Cocoa-
Tree " in St. James's Street was the Tory house in the reign
of Queen Anne ; the " St. James's " was the Whig house   Here
occasionally might have been seen members of Parliament, also
a galaxy of literary stars   This had a more solid reputation
than any other of the coffee-houses except " White's."   " Gar-
raways," or Garway, as the original proprietor was called, was
one of the earliest coffee-sellers in London, and his house was
frequented by the nobility and gentry, as well as others who
wished to sip the aromatic beverage.   All these places, and
many others which might be referred to, were in full activity of

business and coffee-drinking in the reign of Queen Anne
Another notable coffee-house was known as "Squire's," at
which the lawyers and politicians were accustomed to meet
in considerable numbers; and there, it will be remembered,
"Sir Roger de Coverley" smoked a pipe over a dish of coffee
with the "Spectator" But we have been loitering, perhaps
too long, about the old London coffee-houses, and in tracing the
history of *Cafés* in Europe and the East; still we cannot dismiss
the subject without referring to the history of coffee-houses in
our own country.

The consumption of the berry is constantly and rapidly
increasing in the United States, the increased ratio being
greater than the most sanguine advocate of the beverage could
ever have predicted, and pure coffee must soon be so extensively and universally used that all pertaining to its history
will be of interest to the world at large.

In no place in the world, probably, are the influences and
healthful effects of pure coffee more happily displayed than in
what is known to every resident and visitor of the Crescent City
as the old French market of New Orleans. Here, from the
"earliest time," have been coffee-venders conveniently distributed throughout the great maze of stalls and marts, and from
the small hours in the morning until nearly noon the distributers of this most invigorating of beverages are busy as bees.

Aside from their special occupation, these dealers in coffee
are a peculiar people. It seems to be an appropriate vocation
in this genial climate, which at once strikes the observant traveller when he first sees a French or Spanish mulatto, with
her head curiously covered by a gayly striped bandanna,
serving hot coffee. Yet it is a fact that it is only people who
answer to this description who are the most thorough experts in
extracting the delicious taste from the berry, in keeping the
delightful aroma from passing away in the rising steam, in pro-

viding the best kinds of sugar and the most honest and well-
cleaned cups and saucers. At the shrine of one of these ven-
ders in the early hours of the morning, when the fogs of the
Mississippi are rolling over the Crescent City, breaking like
clouds against the intervening houses, and filling the air with
sickly miasma which nauseates the unfortunate whose business
calls him out before the fogs are dissipated, then it is that coffee
is most prized. Look at the recipient, who with blanched face,
dull eyes, and depressed mien, reaches out his hand and seizes
upon the nectar. The moment the fragrance reaches his nos-
trils a transformation for the better commences, the eyes grow
bright, a healthful color and natural fulness returns to the
cheeks, smiles wreath the mouth, the mind becomes active, the
fogs, the dark air, effluvia of all sorts are exorcised like ghosts
fleeing before the penetrating rays of the unobstructed sun.

The European, the Creole, the New Englander, the men of
the West and the far-off Orient, all visit the coffee-stands.
While partaking there is for the instant a touch of nature which
makes mankind akin, for it is observable that the recipients of
the morning cup of pure Java are sociable. Artificial distinc-
tions are discarded in the very act of drinking in the crowded
market, or even standing in the open street. But it is the very
thing, this mixture of the rude and the refined, that adds zest to
the "open-air cup of coffee." The merry twinkle of the eye of
the attendant quadroon, her quiet manners, her attentive observ-
ance of the wants and tastes of the various customers, the very
polish of the tall copper kettle, the jet of steam, the whiteness
of the crockery, constitute associations that, once realized, one
never forgets, and justly places coffee among the most grateful,
innocent, and healthful things that we Americans include among
the necessaries of life.

The coffee-houses of New York are intimately associated
with the history of the city. Within their walls have been the

scenes and players whose actions made the pulses of the nation throb in high excitement, or calmed them to deep repose. The early records show that in 1643 Martin Krigier became the owner of a plot of land on the west side of what is now called Broadway, nearly opposite the north end of the Bowling Green, and built on it Krigier's Tavern. It soon became a resort of the fashionable men of the day, and was at times the headquarters of the Dutch Governor, William Kieft. It was removed in after-years, and on its site was built the "King's Arms Tavern." During the excitement previous to the Revolution, it was known as Burn's Coffee-House, and was used for the meetings of merchants and the associations of "Liberty Boys." On the 31st of October, 1765, the merchants engaged in the importation of English goods met at Burn's Coffee-House, and adopted resolutions to import no more goods from England until the Stamp Act was repealed. Two hundred merchants signed the resolutions. During the same evening a non-importation society was formed in the same place, and a committee on correspondence appointed, comprising many of the well-known merchants of New York. During the Revolution the house became the headquarters of General Gage, of the British army. Years rolled on, and when Time touched the spot again it was changed into the Atlantic Gardens. In the summer of 1860 the ground was purchased by the Hudson River Railroad Company, and the old house was removed to make room for a freight depot.

At the foot of Wall street, still known among the old merchants as Coffee-House Slip, was the Merchants' Coffee-House It stood on the southeast corner of Wall and Water streets, and before the erection of the Tontine Coffee-House, in 1792, was, in fact, the Merchants' Exchange, and political headquarters of colonial times. In 1762 a petition was presented to the city authorities for the removal of the meal-market at the foot

of Wall street, because "it was disagreeable to those that pass
to and from the Coffee-House, a place of great resort." The
meal-market was built in 1709, and occupied the site of the
ancient half-moon fortification and block-house of the Dutch
era.   The Merchants' Coffee-House was five stories high, the
entrance being even with the sidewalk ; a light balcony crossed
the front and side of the house at the second story.   That it
was a business centre in the early days of the city may be
gathered from the following copy of an advertisement in the
newspapers of April 9, 1750 :—"For London.   The Ship Brave
Hawke, John Bill, Commander; Will sail in about Ten Days :
For Freight or Passage agree with *John Troup*, or said Master.
Just imported a parcel of Likely Negroes to be sold at publick
Vendue, To-morrow at Ten o'Clock, at the Merchants' Coffee
House."   A New York price-current of August 6th, 1750,
quotes coffee at 20 pence per pound.   The Merchants' Coffee-
House was destroyed by fire on December 18th, 1804   The
site was afterwards occupied by the offices of the *New York
Journal of Commerce*, one of the most prominent commercial
newspapers in the country.   While the bounds of the city
were somewhat limited,—Broadway extending only as far as
Worth street, and the line of Canal street and Broadway was
so distant from the city that one of the Lutheran churches, to
whom was offered six acres of land at that point, declined the
gift because the land was not worth fencing in,---coffee-houses
were numerous in New York.   Richard Clarke Cook, who had
bought the interest of Andrew Ramsey in the "King's Arms"
on Dock street, near the Long Bridge, reopened it on May 7th,
1750, as "The Gentlemen's and Exchange Coffee-House and
Tavern "   Perhaps the most famous was the City Tavern.   It
was built in the early part of the last century, by the Delancey
family, and still stands on the southeast corner of Broad and
Dock, now Broad and Pearl streets.   In 1757 it was occupied by

Delancey, Robinson & Co., for the sale of "East India goods, shoes, stockings, and shirts, white and checked, fit for the army, with a variety of other goods." On the 15th of January, 1762, the property was conveyed to Samuel Francis, or, as he afterwards signed his name, Samuel Fraunces. He was the Delmonico of that age, having been the proprietor of the "Mason's Arms," near the Bowling Green, the Vauxhall Gardens in Greenwich street, and the great Philadelphia stage-office in Cortlandt street. Fraunces opened the house on Broad street as a tavern, under the sign of "Queen Charlotte." In 1765 Fraunces retired, and was followed by John Jones. In 1766 Jones withdrew in favor of Bolton & Sigell, who were thus advertised in *Holt's New York Journal:*—"Bolton & Sigell Take this method to acquaint the Publick that they propose to open, on Monday next, a Coffee-House at the House of Mr. Samuel Francis, near the Exchange, lately kept by Mr. John Jones, and known by the name of the 'Queen's Head Tavern,' where Gentlemen may depend upon receiving the best of Usage. As Strangers, they are sensible they can have no Pretensions to the Favour of the Public but what results from their readiness upon all occasions to oblige" The house enjoyed a fair share of business. The societies met there as in the time of Fraunces; the Chamber of Commerce held its monthly meetings there until it secured a room of its own; yet the business was not profitable, and in 1770 Mr. Sigell retired from the firm. In the same year Mr. Bolton gave up the business, and Fraunces again took possession. It was during this last term of Fraunces that the "City," or, as it was better known, "Fraunces's Tavern," acquired its celebrity. Large dinner-parties were held there, and among the societies that met in the upper rooms during the winter was the "Social Club." During the summer this Club encamped at Kip's Bay Meetings were held on Saturday evenings, and on the rolls were

2*

the well-known names of John Jay, member of Congress, minister to Spain, minister to England, and Governor of New York; Gouverneur Morris, Robert R. Livingston, Morgan Lewis, Egbert Benson, Gulian Verplanck, President of the Bank of New York; John Watts, Leonard and Anthony Lispenard, Richard Harrison, Peter Van Schaack, Daniel Ludlow, afterwards President of the Manhattan Bank; William Imlay, and Dr. Samuel Bard, Washington's favorite physician. The Club was broken up in 1775. In the parlor on the second floor of Fraunces's Tavern, on the 4th day of December, 1783, occurred the most sadly impressive scene in Washington's history. At noon the officers of the army were there assembled, at the request of the great chieftain, to finally part. The scene has been so often described that it needs no repetition here. In 1789, Fraunces, or, as he was sometimes called, "Black Sam," became the chief steward in Washington's household, at the residence of the first President, No. 3 Cherry street, near Franklin square, where we are told Mrs. Washington furnished her guests on New Year's day, 1790, with coffee, tea, plum and plain cake.

The celebrated Tontine Coffee-House, on the north-west corner of Wall and Water streets, was commenced in 1792, and was the scene of many stirring events in the annals of history and trade. The Merchants' Coffee-House, on the opposite corner, was then called the Old Coffee-House, and its business was gradually transferred to the Tontine, to which place the Exchange was moved from the dingy building in the middle of Broad street, between Pearl and the river, where it had been since the revolution. The following extracts from an article on the Tontine Coffee-House will be read with interest:—

" In 1795 the old Coffee-House was in full operation, but who can tell us of the scenes therein? Who can call back the voices of the old merchants of that day, and repeat the stories they laughed over in the Coffee-House on 'opening night?'"

"At length the Merchants' Exchange moved further up Wall street, and sales of merchandise were not so frequent within the old house, but the long stoop on the Wall street front was still used, an l the advertisements of the day read, 'At X o'clock, in front of T. C., will be sold' ————.""

It was designed to provide a central location for the mercantile community. The merchants had long felt the need of some place where they could assemble and discuss the probable results of trade and the various questions of the time, and during their leisure indulge in a cup of prime old coffee without walking to their distant homes in State street, Bowling Green, and the lower part of Greenwich street. The property was purchased by five merchants, and held by them under the provisions of the Tontine Association as the first board of directors.

"In 1826 and 1827 the Tontine Coffee-House was in the hands of John Morse, who had formerly kept the old Stage-House at the corner of Church and Crown streets, New Haven. He turned the entire house into a tavern, and it so remained for several years. The first floor was in one room, running the full length of the house, and fronting Wall street. At the back of the room, extending nearly its whole length, was the old-fashioned bar. Jutting out from the counter were curious arms of brass, supporting the thick, round, and mast-like timber on which the heavy dealers leaned while ordering refreshments. About the room were numerous small tables, and after supper, in fair weather, around the tables could be seen many of the wealthy city men, diminishing the contents of their pewter mugs, or planning, amid the curling smoke in the room, their operations for the next day. Morse was not successful in the Tontine, and was finally sold out for the benefit of 'whom it might concern.'

"In 1832 it was kept as a hotel by Lovejoy & Belcher, and

was the scene of several brilliant Masonic dinners. The lodges, in annual parade, would march from the City Hotel, on Broadway, down to Broad street; through Broad to Pearl, and through Pearl street to Wall and the Coffee-House—which they thought a long tramp. After the banquet the march would be resumed along Pearl to Beekman street, up Beekman to Chatham street, down Chatham to Broadway and the City Hotel.

Caldwell & Kenyon kept a restaurant in the basement; they afterwards sold out to Charles Ridabock, familiarly known as the 'Alderman.' Charles was a heavy, good-natured German, who kept the dirtiest shop and the best oysters in the city. He had been for many years an employé of George Washington Browne.

In 1823, when the entire block on the west side of Water street, between Pine and Wall streets, was mainly occupied by the stores and offices of auctioneers, a hotel was opened on the opposite side, at Nos. 123 and 125 Water street, by George Washington Browne, and called the 'Auction Hotel.' The host had many friends among the merchants and was well patronized. Some years later, in 1832, the physicians in the city urged all to abstain from drinking beer and wine, and to drink *pure* coffee, in order to avoid the cholera, then epidemic Browne immediately opened a large and convenient coffee-room on the first floor of the hotel, and the wonders of coffee as a sanitary beverage were highly commended. The hotel became familiarly known as Browne's Coffee-House and was a favorite dining-place. A number of merchants that dined there became known as 'the club;' such men as Thomas H Faile, John J. Boyd, Samuel Paxon, Edward Penfold, George W. Blunt, Gilbert Davis, and other well-known New Yorkers could daily be met there. The club has ceased to meet, but the hotel is open, and the coffee-room and restaurant are still patronized.

On the south-east of what is now Pine and William streets,

there stood from the year 1812 to 1830 the Bank Coffee-House, kept by William Niblo. Adjoining it on the rear was a garden, and the building formerly occupied by the Bank of New York, the first banking institution established in this city. Pine street was then lined with the residences of prominent lawyers and merchants. The houses were nearly all built of brick, with sunken areas in front. Mr. Niblo was then a young, active man, taking great pride in the reputation of his café, and soon made it famous for its suppers given by Benedicts taking leave of their bachelor friends. In 1830 the Bank Coffee-House passed into other hands and was torn down, Niblo going to Broadway and Prince street, where he opened the gardens which bore his name.

The cheerful name of coffee-house has somewhat lost its significance in New York with the establishment of the more pretentious hotels, and in them the coffee-rooms are shorn of many pleasant associations. Within a few years a desire has been shown to establish richly appointed and well-ordered *cafés*, managed by *chefs* from sunny France. Those who early embarked in the business have enlarged their establishments, and new ones are constantly springing up in nearly every section of the metropolis, especially on the fashionable thoroughfares, and young New Yorkers have not been long in adopting the Parisian ideas and conveniences of the *café*, as a pleasant place to stroll in after the opera or theatre.

To judge of the estimate in which coffee is held in the United States, it is only necessary to refer to the table showing the annual average consumption to see that we are by far the largest coffee-consumers in the world; six-fold more than some of the States of Europe. Germany and France stand next to ourselves in the rank of great coffee-drinkers.

It is a curious fact, that three plants connect together three different quarters of the globe, which might otherwise have known comparatively little of each other: Arabia is linked to America and Europe by her coffee; China, by her tea; and tobacco has been for ages one of the connecting commercial bonds between the two hemispheres.

Before referring to the various methods of cultivation, it may not be inappropriate, briefly to describe the plant itself. *Coffee*, a cinchonaceous genus, consisting of many species of tropical berry-bearing shrubs, one of which, *Coffœa Arabica*, — the only one which is cultivated, — is a native of Upper Ethiopia and Arabia Felix. This is the parent of the plant from whose crushed berries we derive that delightful aromatic drink called coffee. This albuminous substance — the coffee of commerce — is to that plant what the flour is to corn, the white meat to a cocoa-nut, and the aromatic ruminated substance to the nutmeg. It is a secretion formed in the interior of the seed, and enveloping the embryo plant, for whose support it is destined when it first begins to germinate; it constitutes the principal part of the seed, the embryo being itself a minute body lying in a cavity at one end of the albumen.

Linnæus places the plant among the *Pentandria Monogynia ;* its flower consists of one funnel-shaped petal, with a slender tube, nearly cylindrical, much longer than the flower-cup. It is described botanically as an ever-green shrub in its native state, having oval, shining, sharp-pointed leaves, white, fragrant, five-cleft clustered corollas, with projecting anthers, and oblong pulpy berries, which are at first of a bright red color, but afterwards become purple. The dark-green leaves, shining brilliantly in the sun, afford a beautiful contrast to the pure white, jessamine-like blossoms that cluster and nestle among the foliage; which ever and anon turns fitfully up with the breeze its white under-lining, and glitters like the foam-crest on the ocean wave. Its leaves resemble those of the common laurel, although not so dry and thick. From the angle of the leaf-stalks small groups of the white flowers issue, which, as already stated, resemble those of the jessamine. These flowers fade very soon, and are replaced by a kind of fruit not unlike a cherry, which contains a yellow fluid enveloping two small seeds or berries, convex upon one side, flat and furrowed upon the other. These seeds are of a horny or cartilaginous nature; they are glued together, each being surrounded with a peculiar coriaceous membrane. The period of flowering does not last more than two days. In a single night the blossoms expand so profusely that the trees appear as if covered with snow. The seeds are known to be ripe when the berries have a dark red color.

Travellers and planters tell us that nothing can be conceived more delightful than the appearance and perfume of a coffee plantation in full bloom. The air is filled with fragrance, and the trees appear as if a shower of snow had just fallen on their dark-green glossy leaves, which are almost entirely hidden by the profusion of delicate white blossoms This rare beauty is, however, but short-lived,—for the splendid array of the morning may, perchance, fade away with the heats of noon, or the mellowing tints of even.

Prof Baird, speaking of a plantation in the West Indies, says: "Anything in the way of cultivation more beautiful or more fragrant than a coffee plantation I had not conceived: and oft did I say to myself that if ever I became, from health or otherwise, a cultivator of the soil within the tropics, I would cultivate the coffee-plant, even though I did so irrespective altogether of the profits that might be derived from so doing Much has been written, and not without justice, of the rich fragrance of an orange-grove ; and at home we ofttimes hear of the sweet odors of a bean-field I too have often enjoyed, in the Carse of Stirling and elsewhere in Scotland, the balmy breezes as they swept over the latter, particularly when the sun had burst out with unusual strength after a shower of rain. I have likewise in Martinique, Santa Cruz, Jamaica, and Cuba inhaled the gales wafted from the orangeries; but not for a moment would I compare either with the exquisite aromatic odors from a coffee plantation in full blow, when the hill-side, quite covered over with the regular rows of the tree-like shrub, with their millions of jessamine-like flowers, showers down upon you as you ride up between the plants a perfume of the most delicately delicious description. 'Tis worth going to the West Indies to see the sight and inhale the perfume."

Turnbull, another authority on the subject, tells us that " the fragrance of the gardens of the Tuileries is as inferior to that of the Moorish gardens of the Alcazar, at Seville, as these last —with all the care bestowed upon them—are excelled by some neglected orange-grove in Cuba or St Domingo. Nor is the rich fragrance of the orange-grove to be compared for a moment with the aromatic odors of a coffee plantation,—when its hundred thousand trees have just thrown out their unrivalled display of jessamine-like flowers,—reminding you of what you may have read in Eastern fable of the perfumes of 'Araby the blest!'" It is also amid the prodigal luxuriance and splendors of tropical vegetation that the coffee-plant most loves to linger, loading the atmosphere with its perfumed sweets, as well as regaling the eye with its rare beauty. No wonder that such surpassing scenes of beauty should inspire the poet to such utterance as the following :—

> "Earth from her lap perennial verdure pours,
> Ambrosial fruits and amaranthine flowers
> Over wild mountains and luxuriant plains,
> Nature in all her pomp of beauty reigns !
> Stern Winter smiles on this auspicious clime ;
> The fields are florid in eternal prime ;
> From the bleak pole no winds inclement blow,
> Mould the round hail or flake the fleecy snow ;
> But from the breezy deep the groves inhale
> The fragrant murmurs of the eastern gale ! "

The clustered trees of the golden Mocha in their native soil present a strange contrast, however, with the aspect of the landscape farther northward. "There," states a recent authority, "a low, sandy shore affords a free view over vast treeless plains which stretch in sad monotony as far as the eye can reach, while the cloudless sky sends down an almost insupportable heat; only here and there a limited pasture, with lean grass and a few graceful palm-trees, breaks the mournful uniformity; in the grateful shade a few Bedouins rest under their black tents, while their brethren hasten on the uncouth dromedary through the yellow desert. Very different is the scene on the southern slope of the great peninsula; for here an abundant, fragrant vegetation unfolds its riches and enchants the senses; incense grows like the juniper of our woods; whole forests of palm-trees overshadow the lower parts of the mountains, and vast stretches of durra wave like golden grain in the gentle breeze. This is the home of the coffee-tree."

Amid such profusion of natural beauty rises the graceful plant that bears the berry we so much prize Not only does the plant load the air with delicious perfume, but beautiful butterflies are ever fluttering among its honeyed blossoms, sucking sweets; while locusts are chirping on every branch, and a cloudless blue sky looks down upon the exuberant splendor, till the blossoms fade, and become transmuted in process of time into a red berry, the kernel of which is the coffee-bean. While these berries are maturing and becoming dark purple—such are the effects of a tropical climate—the tree produces a second and a third crop of snowy blossoms, so that the beautiful green pyramidal branches are garnished with buds, and flowers, and fruits, at every stage of development.

Coffee is still cultivated in "Araby the blest," the coffee-gardens there being on terraces which reach to an elevation of about 3,000 feet. The soil is kept moist by means of small artificial canals, which are made to irrigate the whole by the water falling from the upper to the lower terraces. The trees here are planted so closely together that the thick foliage shelters their roots from the tropical heat of the sun.

Niebuhr states that the plant was brought from Abyssinia by the Arabs to Yemen. For ages it is believed to have been cultivated in the hilly range of Jabal. Here the plants are grown in a soil continually irrigated, and where trees of various kinds are interspersed among the plantations, whose shade has a beneficial effect upon the coffee bushes. The fruit begins to ripen in February; and when the seeds are prepared they are conveyed to the city of Beit el Fakih, whence part goes to Mocha, another portion to Hodeida and Loheia, whence it finds its way to Djedda and Suez, for the Turkish and European markets.

Coffee, it has been proved, can be cultivated with great ease and to any extent in the republic of Liberia, being indigenous to the soil and found there in abundance. It bears more fruit there and lasts longer than elsewhere. A single tree at Moravia, it is said, has yielded the enormous quantity of 16 pounds at one gathering. It was estimated some years since that there were about 30,000 coffee-trees in one of the counties, that of Grand Bassa, and the quality of the produce was stated to be equal to the best Java. About the villages and settlements of the Sherbro River and Sierra Leone, wild coffee-trees are very abundant.

If, as it has been computed, there are now consumed annually a thousand million pounds of the precious bean, Coffee can no longer be said to hold an insignificant place among the staples of trade On the contrary, its importance as such can hardly be over-estimated, when it is remembered to what vast multitudes of persons its cultivation, transportation, and preparation for use afford profitable means of support.

There is scarcely any other item of commerce that has made

more rapid progress in the world, or gained for itself more general acceptation with all classes, than coffee. Its constantly increasing consumption as a beverage, as seen by the statistical tables, clearly proves that it may be regarded not only as one of the necessities of civilized life, but also as a very important one. Two things connected with coffee conduce to its popularity,— its refreshing, restoring, and exhilarating qualities and its non-inebriating influence. A beverage that shall be found to combine these essential requisites is, indeed, a *sine quâ non* with multitudes, who, while they would seek the stimulant, would also avoid the penalty of the intoxicating draught. Coffee, therefore, is to be regarded as an auxiliary to temperance; since its use tends largely to supersede that of spirituous liquors. This continued increase in the demand for the beverage, irrespective of climatic influences, will of necessity extend the present area of its cultivation largely into those belts of land which are favorable to the production of the plant. These lands are found lying principally between the isothermal lines of 25° north and 30° south of the equator, as may be seen by reference to the accompanying Map. It has been ascertained that the plant cannot be grown to advantage in places where the thermometer descends at any time below 55°.

Besides the existing countries where coffee is cultivated, there are many other places where it might be extensively grown, such, for instance, as the western coast of Africa generally, the interior ranges of Natal, the mountain ranges on the northern coast of Australia, from Moreton Bay to Torres Straits, &c. Soil and climate are the circumstances which chiefly affect its commercial value.

The cultivation of coffee is now widely diffused over all the tropical parts of the world. It is found in most of the West India Islands, in the provinces of Central America, Cayenne, Peru, Bolivia, and especially Brazil—the greatest market of all. It is widely spread over Arabia, the western coast of India, Ceylon, Sumatra, Bourbon, Mauritius, Java, and some of the Pacific Islands; and in many of these places it is found in climates differing as much as 20° in average temperature. By reference to the Map, a bird's-eye view may be obtained of the several places where the berry is most cultivated or where it may be advantageously produced. According to M. Lascelles, "The coffee-plant will bear extremes of climate better than most plants. In Jamaica it is found on the Blue Mountain, upwards of 6,000 feet above the sea; and in the East Indies it is seen growing, and producing at Coonoor on the Neilgherries, at a similar elevation; whilst, on the other hand, it is also seen growing at the level of the sea in both hemispheres, a difference of average temperature of from 20° to 30°. It has been contended by some that the coffee produced at a high elevation is of a finer quality than that grown in a warmer temperature; this is, however, generally considered questionable."

"When grown at the extremes of climate it is small, generally much lighter, and the actual number of berries is far less than that grown in a genial climate. Experience has proved that from lat. 6° to 12° an elevation of from 3,000 to 4,000 feet is the most suited, whilst beyond this 500 feet of elevation should be allowed for every degree of latitude. It is now an ascertained fact that much of the far-famed Mocha coffee is produced in the East Indies and shipped to Mocha; and no inconsiderable portion also comes from the low land of Kaffa and Enarea, in Africa. The excellence of Mocha coffee appears to consist more in the name and method of curing than any other cause."

A recent authority remarks: "It is often the case that theory is opposed to practice in upholding the idea that there is any substantial difference in the coffee grown in different countries

Where such difference is really found to exist, it will generally be the result of different modes of cultivation and preparation for the market, or what is known as curing.

"The quantity of rain is found to exercise a material effect on the quality of the crop, and a dry climate produces a better flavored and more colory bean than the excessive moisture prevalent on some of the most highly esteemed districts, both in the eastern and western hemispheres. It may be mentioned in proof of the first of these statements, that the size and appearance of the bean have been entirely changed by improved or neglected cultivation, and in one estate in India the beans are scarcely larger than sweet-peas, owing to the proprietor having adopted a theory of never pruning the trees; whilst several estates that had been neglected have improved both in quality and quantity of produce to an extent scarcely credible since they have been manured and pruned. Seeds from Mocha, Brazil, and Java have been tried in Ceylon and India, and the produce has not differed in any respect from that of the plants already in existence there. An excessively moist climate has further a tendency to produce long, weak, elongated shoots, drooping at the extremities, and the foliage thin, the leaf long, but devoid of substance.

"The coffee-tree flourishes in hilly districts where its root can be kept dry while its leaves are refreshed with frequent showers. Rocky ground with rich decomposed mould in the fissures agrees best with it. Though it would grow to the height of fifteen or twenty feet, yet it is usually kept down by pruning to that of five feet, for increasing its productiveness, as well as for the convenience of cropping. It begins to yield fruit the third year, but is not generally in full bearing until the fifth. In coffee husbandry the plants should be placed eight feet apart, as the trees throw out extensive horizontal branches, and in holes ten or twelve feet deep, to secure a constant supply of moisture.

"The berries, as a general rule, when ripe are picked and spread out on large drying-grounds, and are dried with the pulp and parchment on the bean; when thoroughly dry the berries are passed under wooden rollers, or pounded in wooden mortars, and the outer skin being thus removed, the beans are winnowed, garbled, sized and packed for the market. The coffee prepared in this way is seldom so even in color and appearance, but the aroma is better. This method is, however, open to serious objections. Owing to the much greater bulk of the coffee before the pulp is removed, the room for drying would require to be very extensive, and as coffee is very liable to ferment in the pulp, it must be laid very thin, and constantly turned; whilst in the event of wet weather or exposure to moisture, or the equally dangerous alternative of heaping it up, the whole would ferment and be utterly spoiled."

The system pursued by most planters for removing the pulp is by machinery. After being washed and put on the barbecues to dry, it is of importance to keep the coffee constantly turned until it is all surface-dry, and the beans cease to adhere to each other, but it should not be exposed to sun or wind until the parchment cracks, as every hour's exposure to the atmosphere, after that is removed, takes away both from the color and the aroma of the bean. Of course what has been said presupposes that the coffee is picked when fully ripe, since no care in curing or packing will impart color or flavor to a half-ripe bean. For packing, casks or cases are preferable to sacks, since coffee has a strong attraction for damp and for all scents, and its aroma will also suffer by its contact with any substance with which it may be brought into connection. There are said to be ten varieties of the coffee, but only one is found indigenous to India, and it is questionable if this is not the Mocha species introduced from Arabia.

The island of Ceylon is situated in the Indian Ocean, and belongs to Great Britain. Little is known of the aboriginal inhabitants of the island; at present they resemble the Hindoos of the neighboring continent, and consist in part of Singhalese. The Singhalese spoken language is peculiar to this island; but their written language is either Pali or Sanscrit. Ceylon claims to possess historical records dating back some twenty-four centuries, and their authenticity as regards descriptions of ancient towns, buildings, and works of art is established by existing ruins, proving that the island had been at a remote period inhabited by a powerful and numerous people. Ceylon was known to the Greeks and Romans in the time of Alexander; it was also visited by traders in the sixth century, and by Marco Polo in the thirteenth century. Little was known of it, however, until 1505, when the Portuguese established a regular intercourse with the island, being encouraged thereto by the King of Kandy, who first paid them tribute in cinnamon, to defend the island against the Arabian pirates. The Portuguese were subsequently expelled by the Dutch, who in turn were driven from the island by the British. "The total export of coffee from Ceylon in the year 1837 was valued at less than $500,000.

"In 1870 the export was over 94,000,000 lbs., equivalent to fully $17,500,000 in the consuming markets. Within the past fifteen years even the number of coffee plantations in Ceylon has increased from 404 to 1,004; the extent of land planted from 80,000 acres to 200,000, or over 312 square miles, and the crops have generally been favorable. This is exclusive of coffee cultivated by the natives in their gardens, supposed to cover 50,000 acres more. 'Native' coffee is the kind usually exported from Ceylon to Europe, America, and the Australian colonies, and it is prepared for the market after a different fashion from the plantation kinds, which are generally dearer. There are now 1,000 working coffee plantations in Ceylon, requiring 200,000 coolies (men, women, and children from Southern India) to cultivate and gather crops, and worth for the 312 miles of cultivation, together with the buildings, machinery, and stock, not less than $35,000,000."

The most suitable soil in the East Indies for the coffee-plant is that which grows soft timber. The latest authorities seem to confirm the opinion of Laborie, who observes: "If the first (tap root) finds the quickstone, gravel-stone, or clay, the tree will not last long; but if it, as well as the roots, find their way through stony ground, and if there be a good proportion of mould, it suffers no inconvenience, as the stones keep the mould together." The finest estates are said to be of this latter character of soil, and have given consecutively heavy crops, with the assistance of little or no manure. While estates of a lighter soil, having lost nearly all the mould, and having no good subsoil, have to be regularly manured. In a word, a dark chocolate-colored soil, mixed with small stones, under ledges of rock, and bestrewn with boulders, is the best; and the most favorable elevation is 3,000 feet. A level piece of virgin ground, not far from water, where the soil is rich and crumbly, is the most eligible for the construction of a nursery. First the land must be thoroughly cleared, and all but the largest stumps of the forest-trees rooted out; the soil must be dug to the depth of nine or twelve inches, and be made as friable as possible, then divided into beds with narrow paths between them, the seed, in parchment (generally taken from the cisterns after being pulped), should be put in, row by row, about six inches apart. A rope the length of the beds is used for this purpose, stretched from one end of the beds to the

3

other. The seed, if sown in suitable weather, soon makes its appearance above the surface; so that a nursery made in May or June of one year has plants fit to put out at the same date in the following year. A slightly inclined piece of land is more desirable for a nursery, because the natural drainage would be better; and it is important that care should be taken to prevent damage by heavy rains. One bushel of parchment coffee is calculated to yield about 30,000 plants; so that for a clearing of 100 acres, four or five bushels of seed would be required. When the young trees in a nursery have attained a growth and age at which their being planted out as *plants* becomes rather a doubtful proceeding, with reference to the probability of their succeeding and taking root, it is better to make "stumps" of them: this is done by pulling them up, with as little injury as possible to the roots, and cutting them down to about six inches above the root; then to shorten the tap-root by a careful sloping cut; next to trim the other lateral roots, which are often needlessly extended. *Filling in* is the operation that follows holing. It has been ascertained by experience, that leaving the holes open for some time is very beneficial to the soil in a chemical point of view. Filling in, like every other work on a coffee estate, should be carefully superintended. But of all operations in the formation of a coffee plantation, the actual placing of the plants in the holes is the one that requires the utmost care and attention. Early planting is, of course, desirable, because the trees have the benefit of the entire rainy season, and are sure to give a larger maiden crop. The usual course of transferring the plants is as follows: when pulled up, those with crooked roots should be picked out and thrown away; the roots should then be trimmed with a sharp knife, diminishing the length of the tap-root sufficiently to prevent the chance of its being bent or broken. The plant should not be put deeper into the earth than it was, before it was pulled up; it should then be pressed down with the hands or firmly trodden down. A coffee plantation, to be worked effectively, requires to be well "roaded" and drained. Drains, like roads and paths, should be cut as soon as the estate is commenced, or at all events before the trees cover the ground, or the coffee will suffer. These drains are usually about fifteen inches wide and deep, and at the distance of every twenty trees, which would be about 120 feet apart. As weeds are the bane of coffee estates, they are to be constantly cleared off, at least once a month. When the trees have been freed from suckers, and have reached twelve or eighteen months, the operation of tapping is usually commenced. The advantages for the custom are thus detailed by *Laborie:* "First, it brings the fruit within easy reach, and prevents the branches being broken; secondly, the tree thereby acquires strength and vigor both below and above ground, and the stem becomes larger in circumference; thirdly, it affords less hold to the winds; fourthly, the form of the tree is more beautiful; and fifthly, it loses none of its inferior branches, which, as nearer the source of vegetation, are better nourished, and, of course, more productive." Planters have observed that the part of the tree most exposed to the sun and air usually bears the heaviest clusters; therefore the more the tree is thinned out, the more it bears. This is exemplified by young trees in their second and third crops, which bear very heavily, chiefly from the primaries and secondaries. Commonly, coffee-trees bear heavily one year and lightly the next. Regular pruning and searching have been found to produce the most satisfactory result.

The next thing in order is the handling, which should be done twice if practicable before crop. If the force on the estate admits of it, the prunings should be buried in trenches between the trees. They soon turn into vegetable mould, and the loosening of the soil and cutting of the long fibrous roots very much invigorate the trees. In the same manner, the young wood, after the searching, may be buried with great advantage to the surrounding trees. No branch should be allowed to bear more than two, or at most three crops; it should then be removed to make room for a fresh one. As the same wood never bears twice, the branches, if allowed to bear more than three crops, degenerate into mere whips, bearing only a few berries at the extremities. No definite rule can be given for pruning old trees, however; as M. Sabonadière informs us, much depends upon their condition. He states that he took charge of an estate, some portions of it at a great elevation. The trees had not been pruned for some years, and were a mass of thick cross branches and matted leaves; a man might have made a bed on the top of them. It would never have done to reduce these trees at once to mere primaries or parrot-poles. The course pursued was to saw out the cross branches, and open out the centre of the trees about eighteen inches in circumference; then to take off and thin out about half the remaining wood: the effect was wonderful They were afterward handled once or twice, and the result has been a very good crop, on a property which had not yielded a remunerative one for many years. This pruning also seemed to drive away the coffee-bug, and much reduced its ravages. Only during the three or four days of blossom-time is it advisa-able to stop pruning, otherwise much damage may be done, and the crop lost. After the blossom, and when it has set, all the more care is needed to prune with caution, the best branches being retained; while those which should have come off, even if they have crop upon them, must not be left. Sufficient pruning must be done to insure a supply of new wood, and to give health and vigor to the tree to mature its crop.   It has been effectually proved that draining to prevent wash and waste of soil, and a system of manuring while the trees are still young and vigorous, tend to prolong the age of estates.   There is no doubt that, under such a system, coffee-trees may have as long an existence as other evergreens; excepting, of course, such contingencies as over-bearing, attacks of grubs, the tap-root coming in contact with rock, or becoming rotten from swampy soil; all of which bring the tree to premature decay.   For that destructive scourge, the coffee-bug, the following remedy has been tried with great success: namely, —to apply saltpetre in a finely-powdered state, dusted over the tree when wet with rain or dew.

Concerning manures much has been written; but it is found by experience that those are the best which are in general use: these consist of bone-dust, poonac, guano, lime, salts, wood-ashes, burnt clay, pulp, and last, but not least, cattle-manure. Composts should be applied above the tree in semicircular holes, they should be filled in with any prunings or vegetable matter at hand, and then covered by the loose top soil; the new earth from the holes should be used to cover the roots.   The earth over the manure should be well trodden down, to prevent its being washed away by heavy rains, or turned up by careless weeders.   The next process consists of picking, curing, and despatching the crop for market.   When coolies are turned out for gathering or picking they are provided with what is called in planter-parlance a *gunny-bag*, holding from two to three bushels; they have also smaller sacks fastened round their waist, into these they first collect the berries, and then fill the larger vessels.   When fully ripe, the sooner the coffee is pulped the better, otherwise it heats and the color of the parchment is spoiled.   In dry weather it is sometimes necessary to sprinkle water over the cherry, and to let it soak for some hours to make it pulpable; since if passed through the pulpers in a dry state, it would be much cut and damaged.

Amongst other items to be observed in the culture of coffee, the following are of important and practical value. The fruit should be gathered in when resembling ripe cherries; it should then be measured and thrown into a loft above the pulper in a heap. It should be submitted to the first process of machinery, the pulper, within twenty-four hours after, if not immediately. The pulped berries may remain a day and a night, for the process of fermentation; the mucilaginous matter is to be then washed off. In an hour or so the coffee may then be removed for curing: it is there spread out thinly and exposed to the sun, which will in eight or nine hours absorb all the water, and leave the coffee fit for housing When coffee is perfectly cured—which is generally ascertained by threshing out a few berries in one's hands, and seeing if it has attained its horny blue color—it is then fit for milling, which is the second process it has to undergo by machinery. Here the parchment and silver skins are dislodged from the berry, by means of the friction of a large roller passing over the produce in a wooden trough. It is then submitted to the fanner or winnowing machine, and the coffee passed through two or three sieves, when it comes away perfectly clean, and thus, being sized, handpicked, and packed, it is forwarded by mules or railroad to market.

A recent eastern traveller, Bickmore, informs us that in the large wooden storehouses where the coffee is received from the interior, and kept for exportation, the rich aromatic fragrance given out by the berry differs much more than any one would believe from the ordinary fragrance to which we are accustomed. Here it is stored in bags, just as it comes in from the plantations. "In order that I might see what superior coffee the Minahassa produces," he says, "the Resident had several bags opened. I found the kernels, instead of being opaque, and having, as we usually see them, a tinge of bronze, were translucent and of a greenish-blue color. The best are those which have these characteristics, and at the same time are very hard. One of the first plants raised at Batavia was sent to Holland, where it bore fruit, and the plants from its seeds were carried to Surinam, where they flourished, and in 1718 coffee began to be an article of export from that port. Ten years later it was introduced into the French and English islands of the West Indies, having previously been successively introduced into Java and Holland. I am told that it was first brought here from Java by a native prince, and the remarkable manner in which it thrived having attracted the attention of the officials, more trees were planted. There has been a steady increase, both in the number of trees and in the quantity of fruit they have yielded; but yet not more than one-half the number are planted that might be, if the population was sufficiently great to take care of them. With such an enormous yield a large surplus is left in the hands of the government after it has paid the natives who cultivate it, the percentage to the chiefs, and the cost of transportation from the small storehouses in the interior to the large warehouses on the coast, from which it is put on board of vessels, for shipment to Europe and America"

When Arabia enjoyed the exclusive monopoly of coffee, it was not suspected that one day the Island of Java would furnish for the use of the civilized world over 130 millions of pounds per annum. The selection of soil and situation best suited for

the growth and culture of coffee in Java, differs little essential-
ly from that of other oriental plantations. Valleys lying between
high mountains are preferred here for coffee-growing, because
the soil which is washed down from the heights affords fresh
food continually to the lowlands ; the valleys themselves are of
the proper moisture, since the hills surrounding them attract
the rain.

The labor by which coffee is planted in Java and its produce
collected is included among the oppressions or forced services
of the natives, and the delivery of it into the government stores
among the forced deliveries at inadequate rates.

Previous to the year 1808 the cultivation of this plant was
principally confined to the Sunda districts, there were but
comparatively few plantations in the eastern districts, and the
produce which they were capable of yielding did not amount
to one-tenth part of the whole, but under the administration of
Marshal Daendals this plant usurped the soil destined for the
subsistence of the people, every other kind of cultivation was
made subservient to it, and the withering effects of a government monopoly extended their influence throughout every
province of the island.

In the Sunda districts each family was obliged to take care
of 1,000 coffee-plants, and in the eastern districts, where new
and extensive plantations were now to be formed on soils and
in situations in many instances by no means favorable to the
cultivation, 500 plants were the prescribed allotment.

The United States and Holland are the principal markets
for Java coffee, and it is distinguished into pale yellow and
brown, varieties which depend on the curing and the age of
the commodity, and not on the modes of culture or any difference in the plants which yield them.

The pale coffee is the newest and lowest priced, the brown is
the oldest and most esteemed. Coffee stored in Java loses the

first year 8%, the second, about 5%, and the third, about 2%, after which it continues stationary and assumes a brown color. This is the *brown* coffee of commerce.

Recent scientific discoveries have shown that the improvement caused by keeping Java coffee is owing to the evaporation of the caffeic acid, which is the principle that imparts the harsh, bitter, and astringent taste, which cannot be disguised. It is very much the same change that takes place in fine brands of wine, which acquire their rich, mellow flavors only by age. Old government Java coffee has always been highly prized by epicures. Although there is some shrinkage in weight caused by keeping coffee for a length of time, still the great improvement and increased value more than counterbalances this loss. By carefully examining pale and brown Java coffee, much difference will be found in the smell of the raw bean. There is a particular spicy aroma about brown Java that the pale varieties never acquire until age has mellowed and changed their appearance.

There appeared a few years ago a work bearing the title of " Max Havelaar ; or, the Coffee Auctions of the Dutch Trading Company." The author wrote under the pseudonym of Multatuli ; he was an assistant resident of the Dutch government in Java. The book appeared in the form of a novel, and treated of the incredible extortions and tyranny of which the natives of the Dutch Indies, "that magnificent empire of Insulind, which winds about the equator like a garland of emeralds," are the victims ; and how he tried in vain, while still in the service of the government, to put an end to the cruel oppressions that happen every day in those countries. Many considered it an interesting and captivating work of fiction, but the author maintained that it contained nothing but facts, and the government was challenged to prove the substance of the work to be false ; but its truth has never been disputed. It proves that

3*

what was written of the cruelties and sufferings of American slavery, as described in *Uncle Tom's Cabin*, are nothing in comparison to the sufferings from the system of forced labor in the Indies. It is full of eccentricities, and the characters introduced are original and amusing ; among others a Mr. Drystubble is described as the type of a Dutch coffee-broker, who knows all about coffee, and makes his life subservient to his vocation. It bears evidence throughout of having been written by a genius of that order which only appears at intervals, and it serves to throw some little light on the habits of the millions of natives who dwell in the islands of the Indian Ocean, where so large a portion of our supplies of coffee are obtained.

Of late years there has been a growing desire to know more about the great coffee-producing districts in Java and Sumatra. The opening of the Pacific Railroad and the successful operation of the submarine cables have done much to bring about more frequent communication with these important countries. American merchants have not been slow in availing themselves of the advantages in becoming better acquainted with those who have established important houses in the East Indies, and the writer is particularly indebted to Mr. Charles Dunlop, of Singapore, and Mr. John Peet, of Batavia, for much valuable information concerning the cultivation of coffee. Both of these gentlemen recently visited this country, and from their extensive experience they were enabled to give to those interested in the importation of coffee many interesting details concerning the manners and customs of the natives, and how the great traffic with the interior was conducted by their respective houses for their foreign constituents.

Not far from Ayar-Bangis is the port to which the coffee raised in the valley of Rau, in the interior, is brought down, to be hence shipped in praus to Padang, where it is placed in the government storehouses and sold at auction four times a year, viz., in March, June, September, and December. Natal, about twenty-five miles north of here, is the chief port to which is brought the valuable coffee raised in the fertile valley of Mandhéling, of which port Elout is the capital.   Mr. Bickmore refers to a portion of Sumatra where the Musi makes a great bend to the south-west and the path leads eastward over a gently rising elevation, on the top of which is a large and most thriving coffee-garden, and near by are rice-fields which yield abundantly. "This garden has been very lately planted, and yet all the trees that are old enough to bear are nearly loaded down with fruit.   The rice-fields show that an abundance of food could be raised here, and the only thing that is wanting is people to do the work.   The elevated situation of this country makes it very healthy for foreigners.   If any one could obtain a grant of land here, and also the privilege of bringing a large number of Chinamen, he would certainly realize a fortune, for coffee can be here cultivated with little care; and rice, the staple article of food among that people, can be raised in any quantity.   Such a privilege could not be obtained at present, but the liberal tendency of the government of the Netherlands in India promises that it may be, at no distant time in the future.   Such an enterprise would not have the character of an experiment, for the facility with which coffee and rice can be grown has already been shown on this plantation, and the cost of transporting it to Padang or Palembang would be very light.   Sumatra undoubtedly contains large quantities of gold, but the true source of her wealth is not the precious metal she possesses, but the cups of coffee she produces."

Of Brazil, the popular idea seems to have been, that it is a place of mighty rivers and strange-looking mountains, earthquakes, anacondas, alligators, with luxuriant fruits and flowers, palms, with gayly plumaged birds and monkeys. But it is all this and much more besides,—for its climate is perpetual summer, and its scenery the most beautiful known even to tropical regions. The empire of Brazil, although stretching over a territory nearly equal to one-half of the entire South American Continent, with a soil unsurpassed by any other in the world, yet numbers only about ten millions of inhabitants. Like most tropical countries, it does not evince the enterprise and energy so characteristic of the dwellers in higher latitudes. The Emperor, Dom Pedro, is, however, undoubtedly inspired with progressive ideas, although his subjects seem as decidedly opposed to them; an apathetic indifference to all kinds of innovation or improvement holds them spell-bound to antiquated usages and obsolete forms. With a soil so fertile and a climate so genial, all that seems requisite is the enterprise of capitalists, and the application of the improved industrial arts, to render Brazil a centre of greatly increased and increasing commercial importance. The recent abolition of slavery by the Emperor in all Government or State works, by the substitution of free labor, is of itself a great advance in the right direction; and the ultimate extinction of slavery generally will be accomplished when the existing slaves shall have passed away, since their children are born free. When the swift railroad shall have wholly superseded the slow mule conveyance, commerce will proportionably increase, because capitalists and free labor will yield a more profitable return. Rio de Janeiro is distant from New York about four thousand eight hundred miles; that distance, however, might be virtually much reduced by the establishment of more frequent intercourse with it by steamers. Railroads are already in operation, to some extent, under the sanction of the government; and there are others projected. But we have not spoken of the remarkable beauty of the city, and especially of the Bay of Rio de Janeiro, which for picturesque scenery has been thought by some to rival even the peerless Bay of Naples. The former, which is entered by a narrow rocky portal, spreads out into an immense harbor, or inland lake, extending a distance of some score of miles, from north to south. Passing the Sugar-loaf at the entrance of the bay, you catch a view of the vast expanse of water and the distant succession of mountain-peaks which enclose it, and which form a magnificent amphitheatre. They are called the Organ Mountains, from their seeming resemblance to the pipes of an organ. Their height averages from six to seven thousand feet. The name Rio de Janeiro, literally, river of January, which is really a misnomer, it being a bay, not a river, took its rise from the tradition that it was discovered in that month, which is to the dwellers in that clime the hottest of their year. In close proximity with the city is the celebrated Botanical Garden, called Bota Foga, which is rich in all kinds of rare exotics, including the banyan-tree, and has a splendid avenue of palms.

Brazil, indeed, has been called the land of the Cocoa and the Palm; but it may with equal propriety be also designated the land of the *coffee-tree;* since, as we have already intimated, it is the great producing country whence we derive our principal supply of that essential to our domestic economy.

Coffee, although a native of the Old World, has long been one of the most important staples of the New. Meyen states that he even found some coffee-trees growing wild in Brazil, not far from Rio Janeiro, in the woods of Corcovado. It is the great commercial staple of the empire of Brazil, which, beyond comparison, is now the greatest coffee producing country of the globe. Java is the next in order, and although the latter does not yet contribute one-half the quantity of the former, yet it furnishes nearly three times as much as other markets. The United States alone imported from Brazil, in 1871, over two hundred million pounds of Rio coffee. (See *Table*.)

The first coffee-tree in Brazil was planted in 1754, by Friar Villaso, in the garden of the San Antonio Convent at Rio de Janeiro. Brazil was then governed by the Marquis de Lavradio, as Viceroy. The first fruits of the tree were presented to the Marquis, who distributed them among the planters, explaining to them the advantages of adding another valuable article of produce to the country ; but, strong in their prejudices in favor of sugar and indigo, few took any pains to cultivate it, and the progress of increase was so slow and ᐧ gradual, that in 1808, when Don Joas VI. fled from Portugal to Rio de Janeiro, and soon after opened the port for foreign trade, the annual crop of coffee did not exceed 30,000 bags of 160 pounds each. The increase until 1820 was very moderate, the crop then being about 100,000 bags The high prices ruling in Europe, caused by the falling off in production and increase of consumption all over the world, stimulated the planters of Brazil to extend their cultivation of coffee, especially as the price of sugar had declined, and indigo, from its inferior quality, became neglected ; also that much less capital was required for the cultivation of coffee. The importation of slaves at that time was great, prices low, and they were sold to planters on long credits, payment being received for them in produce. This enabled those of small means to buy estates Crops being abundant, and favorable prices obtained, they were soon able to pay off their debts, and establish the custom of credit which was denied to sugar planters, as that staple became unprofitable when brought into competition with Cuba,

Porto Rico, and other sugar-producing countries. It is to be observed that while the cultivation of sugar was declining in Brazil, and coffee increasing and superseding it, in Cuba coffee was falling off rapidly and sugar annually increasing. We now find at the present time that there is hardly enough coffee raised in Cuba to supply the consumptive demand, and the importation of Java and Rio coffees has been found necessary to supply the increasing wants of the inhabitants of one of the principal producing countries of former times. It was not, however, until after the Haytian insurrection that coffee became an object of great cultivation and commerce in Brazil. In 1809 the first cargo, consisting of 1522 bags, was sent to Salem, in the United States, per ship *Marquis de Someruelas*, and all the coffee raised in the empire in that year scarcely amounted to 30,000 sacks, while in the Brazilian financial year of 1871 there were exported over two million sacks

The great importance which coffee has acquired of late years as a staple of commerce, very naturally suggests the inquiry as to the best means of still further promoting its culture   Since the sugar plantations of the West Indies have so largely superseded those of coffee, attention has been directed to other geographical points suited to its growth. Until the era of the French revolution, the cultivation of coffee could scarcely be said to have reached the South American continent; till then it was in a great measure confined to Arabia and the Caribbean Archipelago. Its extreme scarcity during the Napoleonic wars enhanced its price so enormously, that on the first announcement of peace, in 1814, many coffee-plantations were formed on the Costa Firme of South America, along the Brazilian shores of that continent, and even on the southern coast of Africa. Not content, however, with the natural increase of the demand now so universally made for this important berry, France, England, and America seem to have entered into a friendly al-

liance in endeavoring to stimulate yet further the production
by means of premiums for the most improved machinery and
inventive skill devoted to its culture and preparation.

The great coffee region is on the banks of the Rio Parahiba
and in the province of San Paulo; but every year it is more
widely cultivated, and a considerable quantity is now grown in
provinces farther northward. It can be planted by burying
the seeds or berries (which are double), or by slips. The
plants which have been taken from the nursery with balls of
mould around their roots will bear fruit in two years; those
detached from the earth will not produce until the third year,
and the majority of such shrubs die. In the province of San
Paulo and the richest portions of Minas-Geraes one thousand
trees will yield from 2,560 to 3,200 pounds, in Rio de Janeiro,
from 1,600 to 2,560 In some parts of San Paulo, one thousand
trees have yielded 6,400 pounds; but this is rare. In the
province of Rio de Janeiro, trees are generally cut down every
fifteen years; there are some *cafiers*, however, which continue
to bear several years longer. As a general rule they are not
allowed to exceed eight feet in height, so as to be in reach.
There are three gatherings in the year, and the berries are
spread out upon pavements, or level portion of ground (the
terreno), whence they are taken when dry, and denuded of the
hull by machinery, and afterward conveyed to market.

In Brazil, coffee is planted in the following manner : " The
fresh beans are sown generally in the shade of coffee-trees, and
the little plants are taken up, with the earth about them, so
soon as they have reached the height of twelve inches. They
are so planted that the stems are from four to six feet apart.
By cutting off the rankest shoots, the coffee-trees in plantations
are prevented becoming more than twelve feet in height, that
the fruit which ripens in the 20th, or even not till the 32d
month after the transplantation, may be the more easily

plucked. After four or five years the crop is very good, and then one servant is kept for every 1,000 plants. The coffee-tree yields three crops annually, which furnish employment for almost the whole year.

METHODS OF MAKING COFFEE.

It may seem almost superfluous to devote a chapter to the discussion of the best method of making a cup of coffee; but since more depends upon the manner in which it *is* made than is usually imagined, it may not be inappropriate to offer a few words upon the subject.

We propose, therefore, to allude briefly to the many modes which have been resorted to for preparing and making coffee, both at home and abroad. While we do not deny the advantages of many of the following methods, it is believed that the process of distillation, by the direct application of steam heat, as fully described in the closing remarks of this chapter, is eventually destined to be the universal favorite. First of all, before speaking of the manner of preparing the berry as a beverage, we will mention that the leaf of the coffee-plant is used in the Eastern Archipelago by the natives as a substitute for tea. They roast the leaves over a clear, smokeless fire, after which they are picked from the twigs, and when immersed in boiling water they form an agreeable drink. A few years ago the attention of the scientific world was drawn to this subject, in the first instance, by Brande, and subsequently by Ward, in his able papers published in the Singapore *Free Press* and elsewhere. He seems to claim for roasted coffee-leaves a value unsurpassed by the berry itself. "It was well known," he says, "that they had been long employed in Sumatra under the name of coffee-tea."

Thau this preparation contains a considerable amount of the nutritious element of coffee is evident from the analysis; but as the leaves can only be collected in a good state at the expense of the coffee-plant, it is doubtful whether the coffee produced by the berries be not, after all, the cheapest, as it certainly is the best.

In Arabia we find the method of preparing and using coffee very interesting. Palgrave, in his recent work, gives full and entertaining descriptions of the manners and customs of the people and their great fondness for coffee. He thus describes an Arabian dwelling and their method of making coffee:—

"The walls are colored in a rudely decorative way and sunk here and there into small triangular recesses, destined to the reception of books, lamps, and other such like objects. The roof of timber, and flat; the floor strewed with fine clean sand, and garnished all around alongside of the walls with long strips of carpet, upon which cushions, covered with silk, are disposed at suitable intervals. In poorer dwellings felt rugs usually take the place of carpets.

"In one corner, that farthest removed from the door, stands a small fireplace or furnace, formed of a large square block of granite or some other hard stone; this is hollowed inwardly into a deep funnel, open above, and communicating below with a small pipe-hole, through which the air passes, bellows-driven, to the lighted charcoal; the water in the coffee-pot placed upon the funnel's mouth is thus readily brought to boil. This system of coffee furnaces is universal, and this corner of the dwelling or *K'hāwah*, as it is called, is considered the place of distinction, whence honor and coffee radiate by progressive degrees round the apartment; and hereabouts accordingly sits the master of the house himself, or the guests whom he especially delights to honor.

" On the broad edge of the furnace stands an ostentatious range of coffee-pots, varying in size and form; some are very tall and slender, with several ornamented circles and mouldings in elegant relief. The number of these utensils is sometimes extravagantly great; as many as a dozen at a time may be seen in a row by one fireside, though coffee-making requires only three at most. Five or six are considered to be the thing; but when doubled it indicates the riches and munificence of the owner, by implying the frequency of his guests and the large amount of coffee that he is in consequence obliged to have made for them. Behind sits a slave, whose name is generally a diminutive, in token of affection; his occupation is to make and pour out the coffee. On entering, it is proper to say 'Bismillah,' i. e., 'in the name of God;' not to do so would be looked on as a bad augury alike for him who enters and for those within.

" The guest then goes to the master of the house, each repeats once more his greetings, followed by set phrases of polite inquiry.

" Taking the honored post by the fireplace, an apologetical salutation is given to the slave on the one side and to his nearest neighbor on the other. The best cushions and newest-looking carpets have been prepared. Shoes or sandals are slipped off on the sand just before reaching the carpet, the riding-stick or wand, the inseparable companion of every true Arab, is to be retained in the hand, and will serve for playing with during the pauses of conversation. Without delay the slave begins the preparations for coffee, placing the largest of the coffee-pots, about two-thirds full of clear water, close by the edge of the glowing coal-pit, that its contents may become warm while other operations are in progress. Taking a dirty knotted rag out of a niche in the wall close by, and having untied it, he empties out a few handfuls of unroasted coffee, which are placed on a little trencher of platted grass, when all blackened grains or other non-homologous substances are picked out. After much cleansing and shaking the grains are poured into a large open iron ladle, which is placed over the mouth of the funnel, stirring them carefully round and round till they crackle, redden, and smoke a little, but withdrawing them from the heat long before they turn black or charred; after which they are put to cool a moment on the grass platter. Drawing between his trouserless legs a large stone mortar, with a pit large enough to admit the stone pestle, and pouring in the half-roasted berries, he proceeds to pound them with wonderful dexterity, never missing a blow, till the beans are smashed, but not reduced to powder. After these operations, which are performed with much seriousness and deliberation, a smaller coffee-pot is taken in hand, which he fills more than half with hot water from the larger vessel, and, shaking the pounded coffee into it, sets it on the fire to boil, occasionally stirring it with a small stick as the water rises, to check ebullition and prevent overflowing. Nor is the boiling stage to be long or vehement; on the contrary, it should be as light as possible. In the interim he takes out of another rag-knot a few aromatic seeds called heyl, an Indian product, or a little saffron, and, after slightly pounding these ingredients, throws them into the simmering coffee to improve its flavor, for such an additional spicing is held indispensable in Arabia. Sugar would be a totally unheard-of profanation. Last of all, he strains off the liquor through some fibres of the inner palm-bark, placed for that purpose in the jug-spout, and gets ready the tray of delicate parti-colored grass, and the small coffee-cups ready for pouring out. All the preliminaries have taken up a good half-hour. Meantime the host and his friends have become engaged in active conversation, while the silver decorated swords proclaim the importance of the family who are

assembled; presently a large wooden bowl full of dates, with a
cup of melted butter in the midst of the heap, is presented; the
host says, 'Semmoo,' literally, 'pronounce the name,' of God
understood; this means, 'Set to work at it.' Every one picks
out a date or two from the juicy mass, dips them into the butter, and thus goes on eating till he has had enough. The slave
now begins his round, the coffee-pot in one hand, the tray and
cups on the other. The first pouring out he *must* drink himself, by way of a practical assurance that there is no 'death in
the pot,' the guests are next served, beginning with those next
the honorable fireside; the master of the house receives his
cup last of all. To refuse would be a positive and unpardon-
able insult; but one has not much to swallow at a time, for the
coffee-cups, or 'finjans,' are about the size of a large egg-shell
at most, and are never more than half filled. This is considered
essential to good-breeding, and a brimmer would here imply
exactly the reverse of what it does in Europe.

" Be this as it may, 'Fill the cup for your enemy' is an adage
common to all Arabs. The beverage itself is singularly aromatic and refreshing, a real tonic. When the slave presents you
with a cup, he never fails to accompany it with a 'Semm,' 'Say
the name of God,' nor must you take it without answering
' Bismillah '

" When all have been thus served, a second round is poured
out, but in inverse order, for the host this time drinks first and
the guests last. On special occasions, a first reception for instance, the ruddy liquor is a third time handed round; nay, a
fourth cup is sometimes added. But all these put together do
not come up to one-fourth of what a European imbibes in a
single draught at breakfast."

With regard to the making of coffee, there is no doubt that
the Turkish method of pounding the coffee in a mortar is
much superior to grinding it in a mill, as is usual with us.

The fondness for coffee in Turkey is shown by the constant use of the beverage on all occasions, and its exhilarating qualities are nowhere more highly appreciated.

The great luxury of the Turkish bath—now no longer an exclusive Oriental custom, since its general introduction in this country and Europe—has one feature in the Orient that has not elsewhere been fully introduced. There the bather, after the fatigues of the bath, is conducted into a luxurious apartment, where comfortable divans and soft pillows invite him to tarry, and enjoy the "rest after toil," the *dolce far niente*, the "sweet do nothing." Presently attendants enter bearing fragrant coffee served in delicate little china cups, which further adds to the rest and repose from all care, and at once fills the recipient with delight. We need but to introduce this Eastern custom after bathing, for coffee, as already stated, is a stimulant which, unlike wine, does not enervate or excite the system.

The Turks drink their coffee very hot and strong, and without sugar. They occasionally use spices with it, such as bruised cloves, or aniseed, or a drop of the essence of amber But after either method, the process recommended by M. Soyer may be advantageously adopted; namely, "Put two ounces of ground coffee into a stew-pan, which set upon the fire, stirring the coffee round with a spoon until quite hot, then pour over a pint of boiling water; cover over closely for five minutes, pass it through a cloth, warm again, and serve." The chemist Laplace explained to Napoleon the results of various methods of manipulation. "How is it, sir," said the Emperor, "that a glass of water in which I melt a lump of sugar always appears to me to be superior in taste to one in which I put the same quantity of powdered sugar?" — "Sire," said the sage, "there exist three substances whose elements are precisely the same; namely, sugar, gum, and starch. They only differ under certain conditions, the secret of which Nature has reserved to herself;"

and I believe that it is possible that, by the collision caused by
the pestle, some of the portions of the sugar pass into the condition of gum or starch, and thence arises the result which has
been observed.

In preparing the berry, connoisseurs in coffee will, before
roasting, wash the grains and dry them on a pan, placed near
the fire or in a cool oven. While roasting they will stir
them constantly, that all may be equally brown. Some persons
think the aroma improved when the heat is not greater than is
sufficient to impart a light brown color to the bean; others
prefer the coffee roasted to a dark brown; in adopting the
latter, care should be used to avoid burning it. To produce the
beverage in perfection, it is necessary to employ the best
materials in its preparation,—*fresh roasted* and *fresh ground*.
With respect to quantity, at least one ounce of coffee should be
used to make three ordinary-sized cupfuls. The coffee-pot should
be heated before putting in the coffee, which heating may be done
by means of a little boiling water. When so prepared, the
boiling water should be poured over the ground coffee, and not,
as is commonly done, put in first. When a percolator is not
used, the liquor should be well stirred up several times before
finally covering it up to settle for use

Liebig, after describing its properties and the various
methods of preparing the beverage, recommends the following process, which seems among the best hitherto proposed ;
namely, that three-fourths of the coffee to be used be boiled,
and the other fourth infused, the results being mixed. By this
means both strength and flavor are insured. To preserve the
flavor of the ground coffee he recommends that the powder
should be wetted with a syrup of sugar, and then covered with
powdered sugar. The volatile parts of the coffee are thus prevented from escaping. When coffee has been roasted and is
not to be immediately used, it should be placed in a dry situa-

tion, and excluded from the atmosphere as soon as possible, since it absorbs moisture from the air by its hygrometric power, and loses its flavor by keeping. To clarify coffee, the French sometimes sprinkle on the surface of the coffee half a cup of cold water, which, from its greater gravity, descends and carries the sediment with it

The French, who are celebrated for their coffee-making, use various kinds in combination, such as the following: Java, Mocha, Rio, and Maracaibo. These coffees are so delicately and in such due proportions mixed, as to produce a bouquet of aromatic flavors. They sometimes add a little *liqueur*, to flatter an epicurean palate.

Café-au-lait—that is, three parts of milk to one of coffee—is, according to Dr. Doran, "the proper thing for breakfast; but the addition of milk to that taken after dinner is a cruelty to the stomach." Voltaire's favorite beverage was "*choca*"—a mixture of coffee (with milk) and chocolate. Napoleon, it is said, was fond of this mixture.

The "café noir" of the French is coffee made strong with water only. "Café-au-lait" must not be made by boiling coffee and milk together, as milk is not proper to extract the essential properties of the coffee, and coffee must first be made as "café noir," only stronger. As much of this coffee is poured into the cup as is required, and the cup is then filled up with boiled milk. *Café à la crême* is made by adding boiled cream to strong clear coffee and heating them together.

Café glacé is made by adding one egg to every six cups of *café noir*. Sweeten, and put in cream. When thoroughly mixed, place in a proper cooler surrounded with ice. It should be frozen to the consistency of rich thick cream, and, if properly made, will be found a delicious and refreshing draught

One of the most universal methods of making coffee is to put the fresh-ground coffee into a coffee-pot with a sufficient quan-

4

tity of water, which is set on the fire until it boils, and the coffee, if allowed time, will settle of itself—a mode adapted to early risers and those in no hurry for breakfast.

" If you want to improve your understanding, drink coffee," said Sydney Smith Sir James Mackintosh professes that he believed the difference between one man and another was produced by the quantity of coffee he drank ! *

Pope was among confirmed coffee-drinkers ; often calling up his servant in the night to prepare a cup of it for him. It was the custom in his day to grind and prepare it upon the table, of which practice he gives us the following details in verse :—

> " For lo ' the board with cup and spoons is crowned,
> The berries crackle, and the mill turns round,
> On shining altars of Japan they raise
> The silver lamp ; the fiery spirits blaze.
> From silver spouts the grateful liquors glide,
> While China's earth receives the smoking tide.
> At once they gratify their sense and taste,
> And frequent cups prolong the rich repast.
> Coffee !—which makes the politician wise,
> And see through all things with his half-shut eyes ! "

Taken in moderation, especially if combined with sugar and milk, coffee is unquestionably the most wholesome beverage known. In a medical point of view, it has been regarded as a cerebral stimulant and anti-soporific, and an antidote to opium As a medicine, it should be strong, and taken lukewarm.

Coffee, when taken early in the morning before rising, sometimes alleviates an attack of asthma or coughing, and thus proves of great service to many sufferers. Still it must not be forgotten that it is a stimulant, and if taken too strong, or in too great quantities, may give rise to nervous complaints ; and although for a time an aid to digestion, yet, if too freely indulged in, it will weaken the sensibility of the stomach and

* The converse of the proposition would bear rather hard upon those persons whose constitutional proclivities prevent their use of the beverage altogether

derange its functions. Diluents of any kind in large quantities
relax the coats of that organ, and impair its efficiency. Notwithstanding all objections alleged against the use of this favorite
exotic, it is constantly and extensively growing in public esteem
as an exhilarating drink, possessing the good qualities of wine
without any of its bad consequences It is indeed a sign of the
good time coming, that there have been opened in most of the
great cities of Europe such numerous coffee-houses, where, instead of the dram-shop, operatives may regale themselves without becoming inebriates. Even in its early days, an old writer
of the seventeenth century claimed for the beverage this virtue,
when he thus quaintly descants upon its various claims :
" Surely it must needs be salutiferous, because so many sagacious
and the wittiest sort of nations use it so much. But besides the
exsiccant quality, it tends to dry up the crudities of the stomach,
as also to comfort the brain, to fortifie the sight with its steeme,
and 'tis found already that this coffee-drink has caused a greater
sobriety among the nations. For whereas formerly apprentices
and clerks, with others, used to take their morning's draught in
ale, beer, or wine, which by the dizziness they cause in the
brain, make many unfit for businesse, they use now to play the
good-fellowes in this wakefull and civill drinke."

The roasting of coffee in the best manner requires great
nicety, since much of the quality of the beverage depends upon
the operation It is usually roasted in a hollow cylinder, made
of perforated sheet iron, which is kept turning over a brisk fire,
to prevent any part from being more heated than another, and
when the coffee has assumed a deep cinnamon color, and an
oily appearance, and the peculiar fragrance of roasted coffee
is perceived to be sufficiently strong, it should be taken from
the fire, well shaken, and suffered to cool. Not more than half
a pound of coffee should be roasted at once for domestic use ;
for if the quantity is greater, it becomes impossible to regulate

the heat in such a manner as to secure a good result. If the heat be so violent as to burn any part, the whole will be materially injured. The coffee-roaster should never be filled above one-third; for by roasting, the bulk of coffee is nearly doubled, and sufficient space ought to remain to allow of turning the coffee readily, that every part may be equally exposed to the heat.

In Italy they roast coffee in small quantities, very frequently in one of the thin flasks of glass used for oil, which answer extremely well if the roasting is performed over a charcoal fire, and the coffee shaken and turned often. The non-conducting power of the glass is thought to give this material an advantage over metal, as being less liable to burn; added to which, the progress of the roasting can be better watched. One of these flasks will roast somewhat less than a quarter of a pound at a time; and it is, perhaps, worth while mentioning that this mode is often found useful to the traveller.

The grinding of coffee is performed by iron mills. A small portable mill is commonly used, but it is insufficient for the purposes of a large household, as it holds but a comparatively small quantity. When larger quantities are required in a family, a coffee-mill of a larger kind, requiring less labor, is fixed against the wall, the construction of the mill is about the same in both instances, and being familiar to most persons, need not be described. This is, indeed, an indispensable machine in domestic economy, as the goodness of the coffee depends much upon its being fresh-ground. Coffee ought to be ground sufficiently fine, in order that the water may be enabled to penetrate to the centre of the particles and extract those parts upon which the valuable qualities of the beverage depend. When coffee is very highly roasted, so as to develop the greatest quantity of bitter aroma without burning, it is rendered more difficult to grind, for it then acquires an oily surface, which causes the kernels to slip over each other, and hence they are not caught so readily by the teeth of the mill; but the powder, when obtained, is finer than if the coffee had been less roasted, because it is rendered more friable.

Roasted coffee, as before stated, loses much of its flavor by exposure to the air; on the other hand, while raw it not only does not lose its flavor, but actually improves by keeping That the fine aromatic flavor of good coffee, which is one of its chief recommendations, depends upon some principle that is extremely volatile, a little observation will render evident. If a cup of the best coffee be placed upon a table boiling hot, it will fill the room with its fragrance; but the coffee, when warmed again after being cold, will be found to have lost most of its flavor. The fragrance diffused through the air is a sure indication in what manner it was dissipated; and therefore it is evident that in preparing coffee every possible endeavor should be made to preserve this precious part of the beverage. To have coffee in perfection, it should be roasted and ground just before it is to be used, and more should not be ground at a time than is wanted for immediate use; or if it be necessary to grind more, it should be kept close from the air. The best method of preparing a beverage from coffee, or, as it is termed, *making coffee*, is a subject that has received a good deal of attention.

To clear coffee rapidly, a variety of substances are used; namely, white of eggs, isinglass, skins of eels or soles, hartshorn shavings, etc., for it is found that coffee not cleared has always an unpleasant bitter taste In order that the clearing substances may produce their full effect, they should be dissolved before mixing with the coffee. In this manner, with good materials in sufficient quantity, and proper care, excellent coffee may be made, and most of the valuable properties of the coffee extracted.

The difficulty of making and clearing coffee has led to a

great variety of inventions, one of the most noted being Count Rumford's percolator, in which the ground coffee is compressed between two metallic diaphragms, so that the boiling water shall percolate slowly through the mass. There is also the Fountain coffee-maker, in which a body of steam, passing upwards through the body of ground coffee, carries over the infusion, which collects in a chamber.

Another apparatus is the pneumatic filter, by which the percolation of the coffee is expedited and rendered more complete.

Having thus shown the various methods and principles by which coffee is prepared in different countries, it may not be inappropriate to add that Yankee ingenuity has not been idle in trying to solve the problem as to how this beverage can best be made. There have been about one hundred and seventy-five patents granted by the United States Patent Office for coffee-pots alone, embracing every possible contrivance by which the bean can be prepared as a beverage; and while so many are seeking this "arcanum," we find some of the devices both curious and ingenious. There is a patent granted for placing a furnace *in* the coffee-pot; another with curious strainers and attachments to receive the grounds; again another with arrangements to prevent lateral tipping when tilting the coffee-pot; patents for strainers connected with springs attached to the nozzle; others with hot-water jackets, and some with condensers in the lids to catch the aroma; some to hold both coffee and tea, to be made at the same time in different compartments; —and so the list could be continued at length, showing the claims of the many inventive geniuses who have given their attention to this subject.

We will conclude by referring to one of the latest patents, which, if judged from its success and the praises it has received from those who have used it, is destined to become the general economizer and only true method of preparing coffee. Its construction is very simple, consisting of an outer shell or reservoir enclosing a plain coffee-pot, containing the coffee with the required quantity of cold water. This is placed over a pan or receiver which boils water and generates steam. The steam envelopes and completely surrounds the inner pot containing the coffee and water, which gradually becomes heated, but *never boils*, thus perfectly distilling the coffee. By this process the coffee does not become black, bitter, or stale, and can be served at any time, with all the rich, oily, and fragrant aroma of the bean. As the inner pot is air-tight, coffee made in this way is stronger and incomparably superior in flavor to that produced by any other method Nothing is lost in evaporation nor atmospheric action; all the fine aroma and food properties are held in solution, and the coffee is extracted by the action of steam surrounding every part of the vessel containing the fluid. The bitter taste other methods produce and the oxidation of the acids are avoided, and the coffee always remains palatable and agreeable to the taste. This process requires *no* substance of any kind to clear the coffee; the grounds settle at the bottom by their own gravity, after the rich properties of the coffee are fully distilled. It is perfectly pure, and is poured from the coffee-pot as clear as amber, and resembling wine

The infusion is superior as a beverage to that made by any other method yet discovered, besides consuming less coffee; and as it is a simple and economical utensil, coming within the means of all who use coffee, it has the further advantage of having no complicated mechanism likely to get out of order, and difficult to keep clean. If the advantages really existing in the last-mentioned system are once understood, the benefits reaped by all the consumers of pure coffee throughout the world will more than realize the most sanguine hopes of philanthropy in extending the universal use of the beverage so palatable to the rich, so healthful and invigorating to the laboring classes.

ANALYSIS AND ADULTERATIONS.

COFFEE has been analyzed by various chemists, but the results of their analyses are far from being uniform. Raw coffee contains a yellowish-brown transparent extract, to which the name of *caffeine* has been given, and which constitutes the characteristic portion of coffee. Coffee also contains a resinous matter, an oil, or fatty substance, an aromatic principle, and some tannin and gallic acid. Six pounds of coffee give ninety grains of caffeine, a proximate principle remarkable for containing 21.54 per cent. of nitrogen, which is a larger quantity than is found in most other vegetables ; it is a crystallizable salt, of a bitter taste, producing an exhilarating effect when taken in four or five grains, such as is felt when good coffee is drunk. It was first discovered by Runge in 1820, and it is considered by Liebig as nearly identical, if not quite so, with *theine*, a principle existing in tea.

Raw coffee contains about five per cent. of an astringent acid, —the caffeine, or coffee tonic, which does not blacken a solution of iron, as the infusion of tea does, but renders it green, and does not precipitate solutions of gelatine. This acid is changed to some extent during the roasting, but still retains a portion of its astringent properties, and contributes in some degree to the effects which the infusion of coffee produces upon the system.

But the coffee-bean contains about thirteen per cent. of nutritious gluten, which, as in the case of tea, is very sparingly dissolved by boiling water, and is usually thrown away in the insoluble dregs of the coffee.   Among some of the Eastern nations the custom prevails of drinking the *grounds* along with the infusion of the coffee ; in these cases the full benefit is obtained from all the positively nutritive matter which the roasted coffee contains.

It has been found that 1,000 grains of the wood, leaves, and twigs of the coffee-tree yielded 33 grains of ashes, or 3.300 per cent.   The ashes consist of potass, lime, alumina, and iron in the state of carbonates, sulphates, muriates, and phosphates, and a small portion of silica.   According to Liebig's classification of plants, the coffee-tree falls under the description of those noted for their preponderance of lime.   Thus the proportions in the coffee-tree are—

Lime salts	77
Potass salts	20
Silica	3
	100

Coffee contains a considerable quantity of fixed oil and an astringent acid allied to the tannic.   The following is the average composition of raw coffee :—

Woody matter	34
Water	12
Fatty matter	13
Gum, sugar, and Caffeic acid	18
Caffeine.	2
Azotized matter analogous to legumin	13
Saline matter, essential oils, etc.	8
	100

It may be interesting to mention among the curiosities of chemistry, that a most magnificent purple dye can be prepared from the alkaloid of coffee.   It is analogous to the dye which produced the famous Tyrian purple, unsurpassed for its perfection and permanence of tint.

4*

A higher aroma would make the inferior varieties of Ceylon, Jamaica, and Brazilian coffees nearly equal in value to the finest Javas ; and if the oil could be bought for the purpose of imparting this flavor, it would be worth in the market as much as five hundred dollars an ounce. How it comes—by what slow chemical change within the bean, that causes coffee of the most inferior quality so to ripen by keeping as to become equal to Mocha—we do not yet know.

Coffee is supposed to owe its refreshing character to this peculiar chemical principle, *Caffeine.* This substance belongs to the class of azotized basic bodies, and from its presence in two substances so dissimilar as tea and coffee, both of which are in such general use all over the world, it may be supposed to be of no small importance to our animal economy Liebig has shown that the composition of caffeine is closely related to that of various animal products, and that there is reason to believe that it may assist in the secretion of bile. A pound of coffee yields by sublimation, on an average, about 15 grains of caffeine It may also be obtained from an infusion of raw coffee, when certain impurities have been removed by subacetate of lead, and the excess of lead by sulphuretted hydrogen. It forms white silky crystals, which are sparingly soluble in cold water. It has a mild, bitter taste. The peculiarly refreshing and stimulating properties of coffee are developed in the roasting. It has been tested that coffee roasted to a pale brown color loses 12.3 per cent.; to a chestnut brown, 18.5 per cent.; and to a black, 23.7 per cent.

The chemical changes which heat produces in coffee, according to recent authorities, may thus be epitomized · the brown bitter substance and the aromatic principle are produced by the decomposition of that part of the coffee-bean which is soluble in water; and a large part of the caffeine disappears during the roasting It is said that this (caffeine) is carried away with

the volatile products generated in the operation. By roasting
coffee in an apparatus which allows of the recovery of all the
volatile products, it has been ascertained that if it be carried away with the volatile products, it can only be in such
small quantity as to be inappreciable by weight, and cannot ex-
plain the considerable loss which takes place during roasting,
carefully performed.   The loss is experimentally found to
equal nearly one-half of the caffeine originally existing in the
coffee.   M. Wurtz has demonstrated that the lost caffeine has
been transformed into a volatile base methylamine, or methyl-
ammonia ($C_4 H_5 N$). The following are the facts which prove
the change of caffeine into methylamine during coffee-roasting.
"If pure caffeine be submitted to the action of heat, and the
vapor be carried through a tube heated to about 300° Centi-
grade (about the heat which is necessary for roasting), and filled
with fragments of pumice-stone, which delay the passage of
the vaporized matters, only a feeble decomposition occurs; the
greater part remains unchanged, and the little that is decomposed gives no characteristic product except cyanogen   This
experiment tends to prove that it is not the caffeine which
furnishes the volatile alkaloid existing in roasted coffee. But a
very different result is obtained if, instead of acting on free
caffeine, we experiment on caffeine in analogous circumstances
to those in which it exists in green coffee. It is easy to extract
the alkaloid from roasted coffee by distilling the extract of coffee, *made with cold water*, with a weak base, such as lime.
The addition of this alkali to an infusion of coffee immediately
liberates the methylamine, the special ammoniacal odor of
which is readily perceptible."
    In tea the proportion of volatile oil amounts to about one
pound in a hundred of the dried leaf, but in roasted coffee it
rarely amounts to more than one in fifty thousand! And yet
on the different proportions of this oil which they severally

contain, the aroma and the consequent estimation in the market of the different varieties of coffee in a great measure depend.

The action of coffee on the human system is due chiefly to the empyreumatic oil, and consequently is greatest when roasted; but its extractive and also nitrogenous principle, caffeine, must exert considerable influence upon the organs of digestion. " Coffee acts powerfully and peculiarly on the ganglionic system of nerves and their ramifications, and all the organs which are supplied by them. It elevates the vitality of these nerves, and quickens all their actions The brain is also, in a similar manner, acted upon by it; and hence the increased sensibility and energy of that organ during the use of coffee, and the removal of all sense of fatigue and disposition to sleep Upon this depends, in addition to its local influence upon the organs of digestion, the utility of coffee in counteracting the effects of narcotic poisons, such as opium or belladonna; and the favor it has found among literary persons, from enabling them to carry on their studies through the midnight hours without feeling oppressed by sleepiness. It also excites the vascular system, and renders more powerful the contractions of all the muscles, both voluntary and involuntary " Its physiological effects upon the system, as far as they have been investigated, appear to be, that while it makes the brain more active, it soothes the body generally, makes the change and waste of matter slower and the demand for food consequently less. According to a recent authority, over seventeen hundred separate works have been published on that prevalent malady—indigestion—with specifics for its cure: notwithstanding this formidable array of specifics and prescriptions, we are backed by professional authority when we venture to suggest yet one more, to wit—a cup of good coffee, without the admixture of either milk or sugar. It is occasionally useful in relieving headache, especially the form called nervous. It has also been employed as a febrifuge in intermittents, as a stomachic in some forms of dyspepsia, and as a stimulant to the cerebro-spinal system in some nervous disorders. Flayer, Percival, and others have used it in spasmodic asthma; and Laennec says: "I have myself seen several cases in which coffee was really useful. The immoderate use of coffee, on the other hand, is said to produce nervous symptoms, such as anxiety, tremor, disordered vision, palpitation, and feverishness" We find the following remarks regarding the chemical properties of caffeine · "Mulder gave a grain of it to a rabbit; the animal ate but little the next day, and aborted the day after. Liebig has suggested that it probably contributes to the formation of taurine, the nitrogenized constituent of bile According to Lehmann, caffeine in doses of from two to ten grains causes violent excitement of the vascular and nervous systems, palpitations of the heart, and often intermission of pulse, sleeplessness, and delirium."

Dr. Hassall thus describes the structure of the coffee-seed: "Two parts are to be discriminated in the coffee-berry, and the testa or investment by which it is surrounded. The berry, previous to roasting, and even after it has been soaked for a long time in water, is hard and tough, in which respect it differs from all those substances which enter into the adulteration of coffee, and which become softened by immersion in cold water. The hardness is even retained subsequently to the charring, and is so great, that by this character alone the fragments of the ground and roasted coffee-berry may be readily distinguished from those of chiccory It consists of an assemblage of vesicles or cells of an *angular* form, which adhere so firmly together that they break up into pieces rather than separate into distinct and perfect cells The cavities of the cells include, in the form of little drops, a considerable quantity of aromatic volatile oil, on the presence of which the fragrance, and many of the active principles of the berry mainly depend. The testa, or investing membrane, presents a structure very different from that of the substance of the berry itself, and when once seen it cannot be confounded with any other tissue which has yet been observed entering into the adulteration of coffee; it is made up principally of elongated and adherent cells, forming a single layer, and having oblique markings upon their surfaces; these cells rest upon another thin membrane which presents an indistinct fibrous structure."

The seeds, improperly called berries, of Arabia or Mocha coffee are small, of a dark yellow color; those of Java and the East Indies are larger, and of a paler yellow; while those of the West Indies and Brazil possess a bluish or greenish-gray tint. The dried fruits or berries are rarely imported; occasionally the seeds contained in their endocarp or husks, however, are met with in commerce.

The practice of adulterating food originates with dishonest men, who take this means of underselling their honest neighbors in the same business; and it is to the interest of all who prize integrity and fair dealing, to lend their aid in suppressing frauds which so generally affect the public health. Foreign substances, such as we describe, are mixed with coffee to increase the weight and bulk and reduce the cost, and every pound is a direct damage to consumers, who fail to realize the healthful effects of pure coffee.

There are few articles of consumption which have been subjected to more extensive adulteration than coffee. The most prevalent adulteration is that of chiccory; and it has frequently been urged in extenuation of the fraud that chiccory improves the flavor of coffee; but this opinion is not held by most chemists. Persons who have had their taste vitiated by using the two in combination, may even prefer it to pure coffee; but, as Dr. Hassall remarks, " had they the opportunity of partaking of well-prepared and unadulterated coffee, they would not be long before they acknowledged the infinite superiority of the genuine beverage even as a matter of taste."

If chiccory were an improvement when mixed with coffee, it ought to be good by itself; but any one who has tasted the bitter, muddy, and nauseating infusion of this root is aware that only when mixed and partially disguised with coffee can it be drunk at all; between the two articles there is no analogy whatever; besides, chiccory has properties of its own which are decidedly injurious; when taken only in moderate quantities chiccory is not at first injurious to health, but by its prolonged and frequent use it produces heartburn, cramps, loss of appetite, acidity in the mouth, and cloudiness of the senses. It is the opinion of the eminent oculist, Professor Beer, of Vienna, that the continual use of chiccory seriously affects the nervous system, and gives rise to blindness, without any visible defect in the eyes except an immovable pupil.

The ground coffee sold by the grocers is to a great extent adulterated. The principal substances used for this purpose are roasted chiccory and roasted beans, peas, and corn   This fraud may readily be detected as follows:—"A spoonful of pure coffee, placed gently on the surface of a glass of cold water, will float for some time, and scarcely color the liquid, if it contains chiccory, it will rapidly absorb the water, and, sinking to the bottom of the glass, communicate a deep reddish-brown tint as it falls. Another method of applying this test is by expertly shaking a spoonful of the suspected coffee with a wine-glassful of cold water, and then placing the glass upon the table. If it is pure it will rise to the surface, and scarcely color the liquid; but if chiccory is present it will sink to the bottom, and the water will be tinged of a deep red as before. Roasted corn, beans, etc, may be detected by the cold decoction striking a blue color with tincture of iodine. Pure coffee is merely deepened a little in color by this substance. Under the microscope, the presence of chiccory may be readily detected by the size, form, and ready separation of the cells of the cellular tissue, and by the presence and abundance of the pitted tissue or dotted ducts, and vascular tissue or spiral vessels. Roasted corn, and other amylaceous substances, may also be detected in the same way, by the peculiar size and character of their starch-grains."

Chiccory is a wild endive, which is now extensively cultivated in Germany, France, Belgium, and some parts of England and the United States. Even chiccory itself is sometimes adulterated ; as we learn from Johnston, who says : " The coffee-dealer adulterates his coffee with chiccory, to increase his profits, the chiccory-maker adulterates his chiccory with Venetian red, to please the eye of the coffee-dealer ; and, lastly, the Venetian red manufacturer grinds up his color with brick-dust, that by his greater cheapness, and the variety of shades he offers, he may secure the patronage of the trade in chiccory ! " After this little *exposé*, who will not be disposed to prize a *guaranteed* cup of pure coffee ? Pure coffee, indeed, is a rarity. The so-called " Coffee extract " is almost universally found to be nothing but caramel—burnt sugar mixed with chiccory and a little Rio coffee: and this fabrication is the coffee one meets with usually on board steamboats or at railroad stations. The Germans use acorns ground up for coffee, and do not object to the drink. The roasted seeds of the water-iris are said to approach very closely in flavor to coffee itself. Substances mixed with coffee, or substitutes for the berry altogether, have been tried with various degrees of success. Roasted acorns, when ground, have been made to pass for it. The infusion of the lupin does duty for it among the peasantry of Flanders ; also that of roasted rye, one of the nearest counterfeits of coffee ; in the United States another adulteration is dandelion, which possesses also a soporific nature.

There are other substitutes for coffee besides roasted seeds of the water-iris : the chick-pea, beans, rye and other grains, nuts, almonds, and even wheaten bread, the dried and roasted roots of the turnip, carrot, and asparagus.   Also, horse-beans roasted with a little honey or sugar; the nut of the sassafras-tree, or the wood cut into chips; beet-root, sliced and dried in a kiln or oven; and many more; all of which, however, possess little or none of the exhilarating or medicinal properties of real coffee.

Some years ago, it was scarcely possible to procure a sample of ground coffee that was not largely adulterated, no matter what the price paid for it; and in some instances the coffee, so-called, consisted almost entirely of chiccory. In 1850, a firm in Liverpool actually took out a patent for moulding chiccory into the shape of berries; they appear to have been induced to do so in consequence of the exis- tence of a Treasury minute, which did not allow the sale of chiccory mixed with coffee, without printing the fact on each package sold   It has been asserted that in France and other continental countries the use of chiccory is almost *universal*. This statement Hassall regards as incorrect.   He says, "We found that in all the good hotels in France and Germany the coffee served up was genuine, and did not contain a particle of chiccory; but that it was largely employed, either separately or mixed with coffee, by poor persons and amongst domestics, for the sake of economy,—chiccory costing less than half the price of coffee."   The differences, chemical and physiological, which exist between the two articles are thus given: "Coffee is the seed of a plant, and it contains essential oil, or caffeone, caffeic acid, and a peculiar principle termed caffeine; each of these constituents possesses different and highly important properties, upon which the value of coffee mainly depends.

"Chiccory is the root of a plant belonging to the family of the dandelions. It contains no essential oil, tannic acid, or alkaloid analogous to that of coffee. The chief constituents of which it is made up when roasted are a little gum, sugar partly burned and reduced to caramel, coloring matter, and insoluble vegetable tissue." It is evident, therefore, that by the admixture of chiccory with coffee, the active properties of the latter are reduced, since between the two articles there is no chemical analogy whatever. The same authority also refers to this subject of adulteration of coffee with another article named *coffina*, made and introduced, in 1851, into the English market. It was described as the seed of a Turkish plant, which was found to be highly nutritious. On subjecting it to examination with the microscope, it was ascertained to consist of the roasted seeds of some leguminous plant, probably a lentil. Of this article no less than eighty tons were offered for sale by a Scotch house at about $60 per ton; that is, at about 3 cents per lb. " On this single transaction the revenue would be defrauded of no less a sum than $22,200 and the public of at least four times that amount, namely, $90,000. The importation of about 100 tons of lupin-seed from Egypt into Glasgow has led to the conjecture that this coffina was made from it—a conjecture, it is believed, correct."

The adulteration of coffee in some cases alters and reduces so greatly the color and appearance of the article, as well as of the infusion made from it, that the use of coloring matters is frequently necessitated. One of these is burnt sugar, or sugar-house molasses, technically known in the trade as *Black Jack*. Another article, used sometimes to give increased color to adulterated ground coffee, is Venetian red, or some other analogous ferruginous earth. The adulterations of coffee are altogether indefensible; and notwithstanding their frequent exposure, both at home and abroad, they still to a great extent continue to be practised. Some years since, roasted corn, principally rye, was largely sold, and employed to make a beverage which, by a fiction, was dignified by the name of coffee; the chief argument, independent of price, urged in favor of it was its supposed nutritive properties. When it is recollected, however, that the starch of roasted rye is in part reduced to the condition of charcoal, it will at once be perceived that its nutritive qualities cannot be very great, *and that a single mouthful of wholesome bread contains more nourishment than a dozen cups of a beverage made from roasted rye.* The adulteration of coffee by substances so cheap, and, for the purpose to which they are applied, worthless as these, is a gross fraud, requiring emphatic condemnation, and, when ascertained to be practised, meriting exposure and punishment. The following tests for the detection of adulterations in coffee have been suggested: "The means to be resorted to for this purpose are of three kinds: namely, certain physical characters and appearances presented by adulterated samples; the microscope; and chemistry. By the first, we ascertain in some cases the general fact whether the sample is adulterated or not; and by the others, especially by the microscope, we learn the nature of the particular adulteration or adulterations practised. The first means consist in noticing whether the sample in the mass cakes or coheres, whether it floats in water or not, and the color of the infusion. If the ground coffee cakes in the paper in which it is folded, or when pressed between the fingers, there is good reason for believing that it is adulterated, most probably with chiccory. If, when a few pinches of the suspected coffee are placed upon some water in a wine-glass, part floats and part sinks, there is reason to believe that it is adulterated—it may be either with chiccory, roasted corn, or some other analogous substances. The coffee does not imbibe the water, but floats on the surface, while the other substances absorb the water, and gradually subside to the bottom to a greater or less extent. Usually, however, part of the coffee subsides with the chiccory, and a portion of the latter remains on the surface with the coffee; and after the lapse of a short time, in general, both coffee and chiccory fall to the bottom. Again, if the cold water to which a portion of ground coffee has been added quickly becomes deeply colored, it is an evidence of the presence of some roasted vegetable substance or burnt sugar; for when coffee is added to water, it becomes scarcely colored for some time. Lastly, if in a few grains of coffee spread out on a piece of glass, and moistened with a few drops of water, we are enabled to pick out, by means of a needle, minute pieces of substance of a soft consistence, the coffee is doubtless adulterated; for the particles of the coffee-seed are hard and resisting, and do not become soft even after prolonged immersion in water When, therefore, any sample cakes into a mass, quickly furnishes to cold water a deep-colored solution, or is found to contain, when moistened with water, soft particles like those of bread-crumbs, there can be no question as to the existence of adulteration. The general characters of genuine ground coffee are, therefore, the reverse of the above "

By these general means, and without having recourse to science, the observer is often enabled to state whether any sample of coffee is adulterated or not; but, in order to determine the character of the adulteration practised, we must employ either the microscope or chemistry In the case of coffee, by far the most important information is furnished by the microscope; indeed, chemistry affords no certain means for the identification of the majority of the vegetable substances employed in the adulteration of coffee, and, did it do so, it would hardly be required, since these may be so readily detected by the microscope. It is known that the adulterations of coffee are always greatly increased by a high duty on the article, which makes the admixture of all farinaceous substances immensely profitable to roasters and dealers in prepared coffee. It may not be amiss to here state that one of the principal objects of this work has been to call the attention of all consumers of coffee to the pernicious effects of adulterations. Coffee now being on the free list, and paying no duty when imported directly from places of growth, there should exist no excuse to continue the adulteration of so necessary an article of food. If a little attention is given by large dealers and direct distributers throughout the country, in generally informing consumers of the economy of using pure coffee, it is believed that the business in chiccory, roasted rye, beans, peas, damaged ship's bread, stale crackers, bran, and all other such substances used by some coffee-roasters, will be greatly diminished if not entirely abolished. All consumers who once become accustomed to the use of pure coffee will with reluctance use any substitute for the berry, for none has ever been found to possess the advantages of taste, flavor, and the invigorating and healthful qualities of unadulterated coffee.

Some twenty years ago, it was estimated that 18,000,000 lbs. of vegetable matter of various kinds were sold annually under the deceptive name of coffee, while three-fourths of the amount consisted of chiccory. The various substances used in adulterating both chiccory and coffee, when sold in the powdered state, have been specifically pointed out as ingredients prejudicial to health.

TARIFFS OF VARIOUS COUNTRIES.

UNITED STATES.

1789—Section 1, Act July 1, 1789.

    Whereas, it is necessary for the support of government, for the discharge of the debts of the United States, and the encouragement and protection of manufactures, that duties be laid on goods, wares, and merchandises imported from and after the first day of August next ensuing, there shall be laid on all Coffee imported into the United States from any foreign port or place, per pound .. .. 2½ cts.

1830—By Act of Congress, May 20, 1830, Coffee placed upon the free list........ .... Free.

1861—Extract of Coffee subjected to a duty by Act of Congress, March 2, 1861, section 24, under un-enumerated manufactured articles, to pay twenty per centum ad-valorem 20%

1861—Raw Coffee in the bean, by Act of Congress, August 5, 1861, shall pay per lb...... .. .. 4 cts

1861—Raw Coffee in the bean increased by Act of Congress, December 24, 1861, Chapter II , shall pay per lb, gold.... ... . 5 cts.

1862—All substitutes (except Chiccory), by Act of Congress, July 14, 1862, section 8 —on Acorn Coffee and Dandelion root, raw or prepared, and all other articles used or intended to be used as Coffee, or a substitute for Coffee, and not otherwise provided for, shall pay per lb, gold .... 3 cts.

1864—Chiccory root, by Act of June 30, 1864, section II., raw, per lb, gold .... 4 cts.

    Chiccory ground, burnt, or prepared, per lb, gold............ 5 cts.

1866—Section sixth of Act passed March 3, 1866. On all goods, wares, and merchandise of the growth or produce of countries east

of the Cape of Good Hope, when imported from places west
of the Cape of Good Hope, a duty of ten per centum, ad-
valorem, in addition to the duties imposed on any such article when imported directly from the place or places of their
growth or production 10%
(This act took effect April 1, 1866.)
1870—By Act of Congress, July 14, 1870, section 21, coffee reduced
after January 1, 1870, to per ℔, gold . ...   3 cts.
1872—Act of May 1, 1872, Coffee placed upon the free list from July 1,
1872 ....   Free
1872—Act of June 6, 1872, Chiccory root, ground or unground, per ℔   1 ct.
On and after October 1, 1872, on all goods, wares, and merchandise of the growth or produce of countries east of the
Cape of Good Hope, when imported from places west of the
Cape of Good Hope, a duty of ten per centum, ad-valorem, in
addition to the duties imposed on any such article, if any,
when imported directly from the place or places of their
growth or production 10%
Total consumption in 1871, 316,609,765 ℔s

GREAT BRITAIN.

NOTE —The duties on coffees in foreign countries have been reduced to U S gold, per ℔
avoirdupois, in conformity with the United States revenue laws in force at the New York Custom
House

1660—In this year we find the first mention of Coffee on the statute
books of Great Britain, when a duty of four pence was laid
upon every gallon of Coffee, made and sold, to be paid by the
maker   Equal per gallon to. .   ...   8 cts.
1789—Coffee from British possessions . . .. 21 cts.
Coffee from East Indies   . ... 49 cts
Total consumption, 930,141 ℔s
1801—Coffee from British possessions.. ... . 35 cts
East Indies .. . . 62½ cts.
Total consumption, 750,000 ℔s
1820—Of any British possession in America or Africa . .. .   24 cts.
From any place within the limits of the East India Co 's charter 36 cts.
All others ...   . 60½ cts.
Total consumption, 7,000,000 ℔s
1835—Of any British possession in America or within the limits of the
East India Company's Charter, or of Sierra Leone ... . .   12 cts

Imported from any British possession within the limits of the

    East India Company's Charter, not being the produce thereof   18 cts.

Imported from any other place within those limits.   ....   .   25 cts

Otherwise.... ....   30 cts

                  Total consumption, 23,000,000 ℔s

1840—Of any British possession in America or within the limits of the

    East India charter or Sierra Leone.. ... . $12\frac{1}{4}$ cts

Imported from any British possession within the limits of the

    East India Charter, not being the produce thereof ....   19 cts

Imported from any place within those limits   .. . . $25\frac{1}{4}$ cts

Otherwise ....$31\frac{7}{10}$ cts

                Total consumption, 28,000,000 ℔s.

1857—Raw from all parts.   .. .   .   6 cts

    Kiln-dried, roasted and ground . . . .   8 cts

                Total consumption, 34,334,000 ℔s

1871—Same rates   . . ..   6 cts

        Estimated total consumption in 1871, 40,000,000 ℔s.

    The above are some of the most important changes in the tariff of Great Britain.

FRANCE

1872—Coffee, present duty per ℔.. ...   . $5\frac{1}{3}$ cts.

    Coffee in French vessels .   .. .,. . $4\frac{1}{2}$ cts.

SPAIN.

Coffee the produce of, and coming direct from any Spanish

    possession   ..   .. $1\frac{3}{4}$ ct

Coffee the produce of, and coming from foreign countries . .. $2\frac{1}{4}$ cts.

Extract, Essence, and other compounds of Coffee, fifteen per

    cent ad-valorem. 15%

PORTUGAL.

Coffee in the shell. .. .. $1\frac{3}{4}$ ct.

Coffee cleaned. . .   .. $2\frac{1}{3}$ cts.

All imitations, including chiccory, also Coffee roasted or ground $2\frac{7}{10}$ cts.

TARIFF ON EXPORT OF COLONIES.

Coffee from Cape Verde . ...   1 ct.

Coffee from Angola ...   . $\frac{1}{4}$ ct.

Coffee from St Thome and Principe.... . ... $\frac{1}{2}$ ct.

ITALY.

Coffee of all kinds   ..   .   .   .   .4 $\frac{43}{100}$ cts.

GERMAN ZOLLVEREIN.

Coffee, green	3¾ cts.
Coffee, roasted	5 cts

AUSTRIA

Coffee, green	3½ cts
Coffee, roasted or burnt	4½ cts
On all substitutes..	3½ cts

SWITZERLAND

Coffee	3 cts.

BELGIUM

Coffee, green...	1¼ ct
Coffee, roasted	1⅝ ct.

DENMARK.

Coffee....	2⅛ cts.
Extracts, forty per centum ad-valorem	40%

NORWAY.

Coffee	4⅛ cts.
Extracts, forty per centum ad-valorem	40%

SWEDEN

Coffee	2¾ cts.
On any preparation or substitute	4 cts

RUSSIA

Coffee in the bean	3 cts.

TURKEY.

Coffee, eight per centum ad-valorem	8%

VICTORIA (AUSTRALIA).

Coffee and chiccory.....	4 cts.

NEW SOUTH WALES.

Coffee and chiccory.......	4 cts.

NEW ZEALAND

Coffee.	6 cts.

BRITISH COLUMBIA.

Coffee, raw............ ... . 3 cts.

HAWAIIAN ISLANDS.

Coffee .... 3 cts

JAMAICA.

Coffee......... . .. . 5 cts

BRITISH HONDURAS.

Coffee... .... 2 cts.

ISLAND OF ST. CROIX.

Coffee, twelve and one-half per cent. ad-valorem 12½%

ARGENTINE REPUBLIC

Coffee, twenty-five per cent ad-valorem..... ... . 25%

CHINA AND JAPAN.

Coffee. .. .. Free

CEYLON.

Coffee.. . .. . Free

STATISTICAL TABLES OF COFFEE.

Table showing the Imports and Consumption of Coffee in the United States.

	IMPORTS.	CONSUMPTION.
1871........	322,700,479 lbs	316,609,765 lbs
1870	282,540,737 "	280,911,672 "
1869	242,609,255 "	243,441,117 "
1868	238,012,079 "	223,200,937 "
1867.	226,322,811 "	203,506,071 "
1866	165,392,983 "	159,918,881 "
1865	133,574,397 "	128,146,356 "
1864...	145,304,957 "	109,086,703 "
1863.......................	75,269,417 "	79,719,641 "
1862	98,558,680 "	88,980,911 "
1861	182,244,627 "	187,045,786 "
1860	185,779,689 "	177,111,993 "
1859.	248,527,306 "	226,610,300 "
1858	227,656,186 "	251,255,099 "
1857	217,871,839 "	172,565,934 "
1856	230,913,150 "	218,225,490 "
1855	238,214,533 "	218,378,287 "
1854	182,473,853 "	179,481,083 "
1853	193,112,300 "	175,687,790 "
1852	⁁205,542,855 "	204,991,595 "
1851.	216,043,870 "	184,225,700 "

Table showing the Consumption of the Ports of the United States.

TAKEN FROM	1871.	1870.	1869.	1868.
New York	157,842,920 lbs	151,901,952 lbs	148,595,172 lbs.	148,220,831 lbs
Baltimore	88,252,945 "	81,365,543 '	56,731,710 "	39,890,900 "
New Orleans	34,647,550 "	26,116,970 "	19,676,312 "	17,248,880 "
Boston	9,227,700 "	8,394,560 "	6,457,963 "	4,705,046 "
Philadelphia	5,441,130 "	1,941,945 "	4,347,420 "	8,030,360 "
Other Ports	21,197,520 "	11,190,700 "	7,632,540 "	5,104,920 "
Total	316,609,765 "	280,911,672 "	243,441,117 "	223,200,937 '

Increase 1871 over 1870	.	35,698,093 lbs.
" 1870 " 1869	. .	37,470,555 "
" 1869 " 1868 .	.	20,240,180 "
Total increase three years	. .	93,408,828 lbs.

Table showing the Consumption of the various kinds of Coffee in the United States for the year 1871.

Of Brazil	244,809,600 lbs
Of Java, Sumatra, and Singapore, including receipts direct and from Europe	27,776,000 "
Of Maracaibo.	14,784,000 "
Of Laguayra	8,064,000 "
Of Ceylon	5,824,000 "
Of St Domingo	4,144,000 "
Of Other West Indies	4,480,000 "
Of Central American, Mexican, and other foreign.	6,728,165 "
	316,600,765 lbs.

Table showing the Shipments of Coffee from the Ports of Rio de Janeiro and Santos.

		UNITED STATES	EUROPE	ELSEWHERE
From Rio de Janeiro	1871-2	172,804,960 lbs	89,364,160 lbs	10,701,440 lbs.
" " "	1870-1	238,106,880 "	157,110,080 "	10,380,000 "
" " "	1869-70..	186,206,480 "	125,391,520 "	11,347,200 "
From Santos	1871-2 .	12,825,440 "	41,620,080 "	
'	1870-1	12,288,160 "	50,178,080 "	
"	1869-70	13,334,400 "	64,777,600 "	

Table showing the yearly average Prices of Coffee at New York.

	1871	1870.	1869.
Brazil, Fair to Prime Cargoes .	15 $\frac{?}{100}$ per. lb	16 $\frac{43}{100}$ per. lb	15 $\frac{82}{100}$ per. lb
Java, Bags and Mats . .	21 $\frac{29}{100}$ "	21 $\frac{19}{100}$ "	23 $\frac{2}{100}$ "
Maracaibo and Laguayra .	16 $\frac{22}{100}$ "	17 $\frac{47}{100}$ "	17 $\frac{54}{100}$ "
St. Domingo . . .	13 $\frac{55}{100}$ "	14 $\frac{83}{100}$.	14 $\frac{80}{100}$ "

Lightning Source UK Ltd.
Milton Keynes UK
UKHW022121060223
416578UK00004B/631